DURHAM

doorway to discovery

In celebration of Durham!

Linda S. Baggli

DURHAM
doorway to discovery

Written by LINDA SURRATT ROGGLI

Profiles by LINDA SURRATT ROGGLI & KAY MCLAIN

Featuring the Photography of PAUL H. LIGGITT

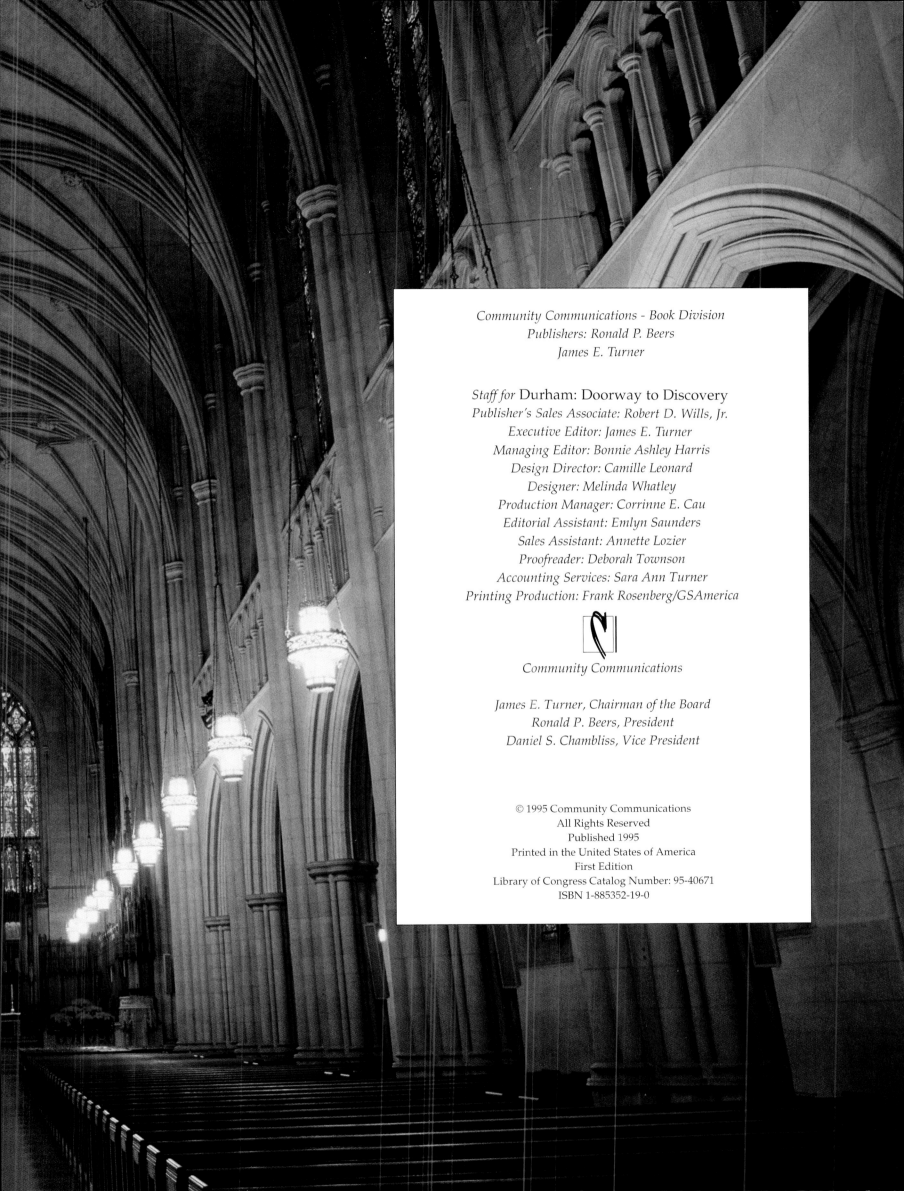

Community Communications - Book Division
Publishers: Ronald P. Beers
James E. Turner

Staff for Durham: Doorway to Discovery
Publisher's Sales Associate: Robert D. Wills, Jr.
Executive Editor: James E. Turner
Managing Editor: Bonnie Ashley Harris
Design Director: Camille Leonard
Designer: Melinda Whatley
Production Manager: Corrinne E. Cau
Editorial Assistant: Emlyn Saunders
Sales Assistant: Annette Lozier
Proofreader: Deborah Townson
Accounting Services: Sara Ann Turner
Printing Production: Frank Rosenberg/GSAmerica

Community Communications

James E. Turner, Chairman of the Board
Ronald P. Beers, President
Daniel S. Chambliss, Vice President

contents–part one
foreword, page 8; preface, page 10

contents–part two
durham's enterprises

FOREWORD

From the tip of its tallest skyscraper to the bottom of its
deepest lake, Durham fosters discovery. Some of these discoveries make
international headlines: the creation of Astroturf, the invention of
the first cigarette-rolling machine, the success of the AIDS treatment,
AZT. These and hundreds of other discoveries—old and new, large and
small—permeate the very fiber of Durham, creating
an aura of possibility. For those of us fortunate enough to live here,
Durham's nurturing atmosphere reassures us of our rich opportunities;
for newcomers and visitors, it is a beacon call to join us. While we
make no claim to perfection—we struggle with our challenges
just as others do—Durham's tenacious spirit of discovery is
what makes our community unique in all the world.
Over the years, Durham has embraced a host of slogans:
the City of Medicine, the Bull City, the City of Research, the Diet
Capital of the World. Today, I offer yet another moniker,
Durham: Doorway to Discovery, as the title to Durham's
inaugural showcase book. In vivid photographs and eloquent prose, this
book touches each of Durham's fascinating (and considerable) assets.
It is a sweep of information that encompasses Durham's
social, economic and political life from yesteryear to present day.
And, it offers a glimpse into real life in Durham, NC.
As author Linda Surratt Roggli writes, "Durham is simply a
nice place to live." We couldn't agree more.
So it is with a great deal of pride that I, on behalf of the
Board of Directors of the Greater Durham Chamber of Commerce,
present **Durham: Doorway to Discovery**. It is our sincere hope that
these pages will remind natives and show newcomers the many
miracles that are Durham. Savor these words, revisit these pictures.
They can become your guide as you "discover Durham" for yourself.

— *Robert H. Booth*
President/CEO, Greater Durham Chamber of Commerce, 1995

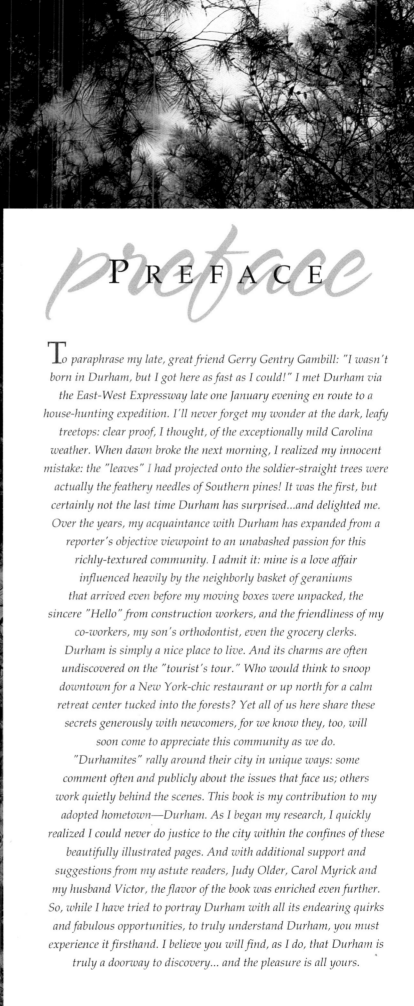

PREFACE

To paraphrase my late, great friend Gerry Gentry Gambill: "I wasn't born in Durham, but I got here as fast as I could!" I met Durham via the East-West Expressway late one January evening en route to a house-hunting expedition. I'll never forget my wonder at the dark, leafy treetops: clear proof, I thought, of the exceptionally mild Carolina weather. When dawn broke the next morning, I realized my innocent mistake: the "leaves" I had projected onto the soldier-straight trees were actually the feathery needles of Southern pines! It was the first, but certainly not the last time Durham has surprised...and delighted me. Over the years, my acquaintance with Durham has expanded from a reporter's objective viewpoint to an unabashed passion for this richly-textured community. I admit it: mine is a love affair influenced heavily by the neighborly basket of geraniums that arrived even before my moving boxes were unpacked, the sincere "Hello" from construction workers, and the friendliness of my co-workers, my son's orthodontist, even the grocery clerks. Durham is simply a nice place to live. And its charms are often undiscovered on the "tourist's tour." Who would think to snoop downtown for a New York-chic restaurant or up north for a calm retreat center tucked into the forests? Yet all of us here share these secrets generously with newcomers, for we know they, too, will soon come to appreciate this community as we do. "Durhamites" rally around their city in unique ways: some comment often and publicly about the issues that face us; others work quietly behind the scenes. This book is my contribution to my adopted hometown—Durham. As I began my research, I quickly realized I could never do justice to the city within the confines of these beautifully illustrated pages. And with additional support and suggestions from my astute readers, Judy Older, Carol Myrick and my husband Victor, the flavor of the book was enriched even further. So, while I have tried to portray Durham with all its endearing quirks and fabulous opportunities, to truly understand Durham, you must experience it firsthand. I believe you will find, as I do, that Durham is truly a doorway to discovery... and the pleasure is all yours.

— Linda Surratt Roggli

PART ONE
doorway to discovery

chapter one
INTRODUCTION & HISTORY

Listen closely to the high-tech hum
of life in Durham and in the simmering
undercurrent, you might catch a whisper of its
rich heritage—the voices of the visionary
men and women who laid its foundation.
They echo the chant of the tobacco auctioneer,
the cadence of the textile looms, and the
rhythm of the Durham blues.

Duke Homestead, home of tobacco magnate Washington Duke, who tramped home from the Civil War to tell his children, "The war is over. For people who will do their duty and stick to their business, there was never a better opportunity in the world for men to make their fortunes." Photo by Bob Hopkins/Impact Photography.

Their voices sing the refrain of Durham's unshakable moorings: an honest day's work for an honest day's pay. They rejoice at the entrepreneurial spirit that has given rise to Durham's extraordinary transformation from yesteryear's railroad whistle stop to today's international center for research, medicine, and education. They celebrate the essence of Durham—the wonder of its natural beauty, the strength of its culture, the electric diversity of its people.

From the peak of Red Mountain in the north to the water's edge of Jordan Lake in the south, Durham-and-Durham-County (spoken quickly in the same breath, since there is only one incorporated municipality in the county) spans 296 square miles of central North Carolina's most beautiful terrain. Dense pine and hardwood forests tower overhead. Rolling hills and rushing rivers provide stunning vistas. An uncommonly mild climate affords even the die-hard golfer or hiker 365-day-a-year opportunities. These assets are among the star attractions for the nearly 200,000 residents of the county, three-quarters of whom live within the city limits.

Durham residents—natives and move-ins—come in virtually every size, shape, color, nationality, age, gender, and philosophy. Here, artisans rub elbows with lab technicians and physicians tutor schoolchildren. "We have a unique population," says Durham Mayor Sylvia Kerckhoff. "There's a little bit of everything—all the pieces we need to make a wonderful big quilt!"

The quilt created by this populace encompasses an impressive array of institutions that call Durham "home"—also on the star attractions list: Duke University, the American Dance Festival, the North Carolina School of Science and Mathematics, North Carolina Central University, the Museum of Life and Science, the Carolina Theatre, the Durham Bulls, and of course, the lion's share of Research Triangle Park—the largest restricted research park in the United States.

"The Park," as it is affectionately known to locals, is the outgrowth of the considerable brainpower shared between three nationally ranked research universities—Duke, the University of North Carolina at Chapel Hill, and North Carolina State University in Raleigh. The Park, centered in an area now dubbed "the Triangle," was carefully planned to preserve the ambience of the heavily wooded area, while encouraging the most sophisticated corporate presence. The combination is a magnet not only for top companies, but for a highly educated work force that often comes for a visit (or a degree or a job) and stays for a lifetime.

Outstanding quality of life factors—the low cost of living, plentiful housing, forested natural resources, notable schools, and low unemployment—have won the region a dizzying array of national accolades. The Triangle was recently named the "Best Place to Live in America" (*Money* magazine) and the "Best Place in America for Business" for knowledge workers (*Fortune* magazine). It is consistently ranked among the top 10 for housing, business startups, international business, and medical care.

A minor flaw in the rankings is that national polls tend to treat the Triangle's triumvirate of cities as a single entity—three homogenous cities growing slowly together. As anyone living here will tell you, nothing could be further from the truth. While the three cities work hard at cooperation, the region clearly shares resources: each city offers unique gifts to the equation. As the state capital, Raleigh tends to be a government town; Chapel Hill's energy revolves around the university. Durham, perched at the apex of the Triangle, is renowned not only as the City of Education, the Bull City, and the City of Medicine, it is well-known as a multifaceted community that reflects miraculous diversity.

Dr. Bartlett S. Durham, a country physician, was named founder of Durham in recognition of his gift of four acres of prime property to the North Carolina Railroad Company. "Durham Station" was later called Durhamville, Durham Depot, and finally Durham. Photos by Paul Liggitt Photography.

It has always been so. Even sketchy archaeological evidence suggests the present-day Durham County was a popular place to live as early as 10,000 B.C.! The towering virgin forests and clear-water streams attracted a proud parade of ancient Indian tribes who hunted and farmed the verdant region.

By the time England lay claim to North Carolina as one of its original 13 colonies, the Indians traversed a well-established Trading Path that cut a swath through northern Durham County as it swept from Virginia to Georgia. Although it was officially a part of Orange County at the time, present-day Durham County was first settled by Europeans who moved in from the north—disgruntled Virginians in search of a better life. They promptly dubbed the region "the Flower of Carolina."

Painstakingly, the hardy settlers felled the giant Southern pines and set out to farm the Piedmont clay. On the banks of the Eno, the Little, and the Flat rivers, they built mills to grind their raw wheat and corn into grist for food. And they traded along the rivers, the rudimentary roads, and along the great Indian Trading Path.

Word of the riches to be found in the Flower of Carolina spread quickly. More and more settlers staked claims and soon large landowners created plantations. With Hardscrabble, Fairntosh, and Stagville plantations devouring prime farmland in northern Durham County, urban development was forced to the south, the lower shelf of the Durham County geography.

A few ambitious souls soon established travelers trading posts and rest stops across the midsection of the county. The proprietor of one such stop—and undoubtedly the most famous —was William N. Pratt of Prattsburg, who quite nearly changed the course of Durham's history.

Prattsburg was a rough-and-tumble, rowdy rest stop, thanks to Pratt's exuberance. Even when he was hauled into court, accused of encouraging scurrilous behaviors such as drinking, cursing, and fighting, he took it in stride. So when the North Carolina Railroad Company needed a small bit of Pratt's land as right-of-way for their newfangled iron horse that would soon chug across the state, it was

no surprise that Pratt balked, worrying that the loud engines would scare the horses of his steady customers. He hiked his selling price sky-high, and railroad officials backed off.

Into the fray stepped Dr. Bartlett Durham, a physician who had recently purchased 100 acres of land directly in the path of the proposed railway. In May, 1852, he offered the company four prime acres, and Durham Station was born. Later called Durhamville, Durham Depot, and finally Durham, the little town grew quickly.

Fewer than 10 years later, with a population of 100, and three stores to its name, Durham turned to manufacturing. Banking on the increasing popularity of "bright leaf" tobacco, an enterprising entrepreneur opened Durham's first tobacco processing factory. A happy accident of Durham's poor clay soil and heavy rains, "bright leaf" tobacco produced a mild smoke that would seal Durham's fortunes in the post-Civil War world.

It had been Durham's good fortune to escape the fighting in the bitter clash between North and South (possibly because North Carolina had been the very last state to secede from the Union), but it would not escape the truce. The Army of Northern Virginia had surrendered at Appomattox, but the rest of the war raged on when Union General William Sherman marched into Raleigh in the spring of 1865. He faced off against Confederate General Joseph Johnston, who was camped in Hillsborough. Rather than engage in battle, Sherman proposed an armistice—the largest surrender of Confederate troops in the war. Johnston, war-weary, agreed. On the morning after Lincoln was assassinated—April 17—the two generals met at a point midway between their troops—humble Bennitt farmhouse (now spelled Bennett) in present-day Durham.

While the generals ironed out the agreement, their soldiers shared stories and smokes in the "neutral zone"—John Green's tobacco factory. By the time the treaty was signed, the tobacco was gone, looted by the soldiers. Green resigned himself to financial ruin until reorders for his "bright tobacco" began pouring in from

A happy accident of Durham's poor clay soil and heavy rains, "bright leaf" tobacco produced a mild smoke that would seal Durham's fortunes in the post-Civil War world. Photo by Paul Liggitt Photography.

17

Actors portraying Confederate General Joseph Johnston and Union General William Sherman about to participate in the annual Bennett Place reenactment. Photo by Paul Liggitt Photography.

The first successful cigarette-rolling machinery was introduced in Durham. Photo by Paul Liggitt Photography.

Fairntosh Plantation. Photo by Rick Alexander & Associates.

across the country. The former soldiers were hooked on the mellow smokes. Green quickly brought his factory back up to full production and began packaging "Bull Durham" tobacco for distribution nationwide. Although Green met an untimely death, his Bull Durham legacy was carried forth by his partner, William T. Blackwell, and ultimately by the generous spirit of General Julian S. Carr.

It was Carr's advertising genius that plastered the distinctive Bull Durham logo in ballparks, on barns, even on the Great Sphinx in Egypt, spawning new vernacular, such as "the bullpen" and "shooting the bull." In Durham, the Bull Durham factory even featured a Bull whistle that reverberated through downtown several times a day!

The lessons of Bull Durham's post-war prosperity had not been lost on other returning warriors. Washington Duke, a 45-year-old Confederate veteran, tramped home to his plain homestead and told his children, "The war is over. For people who will do their duty and stick to their business, there was never a better opportunity in the world for men to make their fortunes." Duke and his children built their own tobacco empire, spurred by the good business sense of Duke's youngest son, James, and the financial backing of the George W. Watts family.

Intrigued by a new tobacco product called "cigarettes," Duke began production in Durham, quickly introduced the first successful cigarette-rolling machinery, and opened another plant in New York. He then convinced his four major New York competitors to sell out to him in exchange for large blocks of stock in his new firm. In 1890, at age 33, James B. Duke was named president of the $25 million American Tobacco Company—the same company that was later dissected by the federal courts for violating antitrust laws.

The dawning of the Industrial Age was embraced by other businessmen in Durham, too. General Carr diversified by financing the Golden Belt Manufacturing Plant—the first of many textile plants that would pump additional life into Durham's already-robust economy. Durham's Erwin Mills once held the distinction as the largest manufacturer of denim in the country, and no factory in the world produced as much hosiery as the Durham Hosiery Mill. The mills held Durham in good stead, with the creation of jobs, construction of mill houses, and a consistent source of revenue, until the 1980s, when foreign competition and plummeting profits closed their doors. A similar fate befell the tobacco companies as health warnings replaced tobacco remedies. Today, only Liggett & Myers' lone tobacco factory sends the sweet syrupy aroma of tobacco wafting downwind through downtown Durham on fall days.

Durham was finally incorporated as a town in 1869, but it took a dozen years to convince Orange County to let go of a narrow rib to create Durham County—a roughly rectangular area about 25 miles long and 16 miles wide at its broadest point. Now the city could conduct its own legal business instead of trekking to Hillsborough.

▌ General Julian S. Carr. Courtesy of Duke University Archives, Durham, NC.

▌ Downtown Durham was electric with the bustle of tobacco and trains in the early 1900s. Photo by Bob Hopkins/Impact Photography, Courtesy of Brightleaf Square Collection.

And conduct business, it did! The thriving economy of downtown Durham was reflected in the adjacent growing black community nicknamed "Hayti." Settled by freed men at the end of the war, Hayti became a hotbed for new business starts. The nation's first black-owned insurance firm was created in Hayti, the brainchild of black businessman John Merrick and Dr. Aaron Moore, Durham's first black physician. When super-salesman C.C. Spaulding joined the firm, aspirations for the North Carolina Mutual and Provident Association (now NC Mutual Life Insurance Co.) went into high gear. It soon had enough capital to erect its own building on Parrish Street—the foundation of the "Black Wall Street." NC Mutual's success launched Mechanics and Farmers Bank (Durham's first black bank), the Bull City Drug Store, clothing stores, tailoring and barber shops, a newspaper, and a host of support businesses. News of the astonishing feat reached Booker T. Washington, who visited Durham in a show of support for black enterprise.

At the turn of the century, Durham was the wealthiest city in the state. Mansions erupted from Durham's clay soil. The elegant Southern Conservatory of Music brought culture into the city. But something was still missing—an institution of higher learning. The proud little town had been bruised by the rebuff of the Baptist Female University (now Meredith College), which chose Raleigh as its home, sniffing that "Durham was no fit place for innocent girls to abide, even surrounded by college walls." Chapel Hill already had the nation's first state-supported university. Durham desperately wanted an infusion of education.

It came in 1887 when competing tobacco magnates Washington Duke and Julian Carr enticed tiny Trinity College to pack all its belongings into a single railroad boxcar and move from Randolph County to Durham, 70 miles away. The college struggled financially for years, but in 1924 Trinity became

Duke University under conditions of a $40 million bequest to the school from James B. Duke. The endowment doubled after his death, leading to the creation of a full complement of professional schools, including a Divinity School, Law School, and internationally acclaimed Medical School and Medical Center.

In Hayti, Dr. James Shepard envisioned the National Religious Training School and Chautauqua as a training ground for black Sunday School teachers. His idea quickly expanded to include academic classes, and with a gift from Benjamin Newton Duke, James Duke's older brother, the school was established on 30 acres on Fayetteville Street. It, too, faced serious financial obstacles until it became a part of the State's University of North Carolina System. Today the state school operates as North Carolina Central University (NCCU).

Students at North Carolina College (the forerunner of NCCU) played a substantial role in Durham's civil rights history. Although the town's thriving black economy produced an affluent, well-educated black middle class, it was, after all, the age of segregation. In Durham, as elsewhere across the nation, black and white residents led parallel, politely separate lives. When black frustrations with this arrangement grew beyond tolerance, Durham leaders began the determined process of integration.

"Sit-ins," a 1960s nonviolent protest technique that gained national prominence, were launched in Durham in 1957 when Rev. Douglas Moore and a group of NCCU students were refused service from the Royal Ice Cream Company. Members of the group simply sat down quietly, awaiting their inevitable arrest. Though Durham had a long history of black political activism, especially

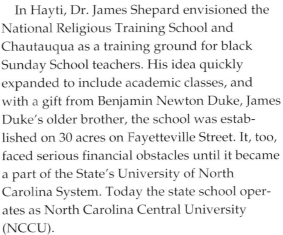

Office of North Carolina Mutual and Provident Association (after 1919, the North Carolina Mutual Life Insurance Company). From left, Dr. Aaron McDuffie Moore, John M. Avery, John Merrick, Edward Merrick, and Charles Clinton Spaulding. Courtesy of Durham County Library, DHPA.

through the Durham Committee on the Affairs of Black People, by the time the integration dust settled, it could finally enjoy the social freedom activism had wrought.

Durham's health care legacy got its start in 1895, when George Watts built Durham's first hospital at a cost of $30,000. Viewed with suspicion by townspeople as a place to go to die, all but four of the rooms were offered free. Attitudes shifted, however, and soon the four-building complex was inadequate for its growing task. Watts came to the rescue again with a larger hospital (now used for the NC School of Science and Mathematics) completed in 1909. The hospital, however, admitted only white patients.

To remedy the situation, Dr. Aaron Moore teamed up with John Merrick once again to create Lincoln Hospital, the city's first black medical facility, in the early 1900s. When the new, integrated Durham County Hospital was built in the 1970s, Watts was closed and Lincoln became an outpatient clinic—Lincoln Community Health Center. With these two public medical facilities, Duke University Medical Center, the Durham Veterans Administration Hospital, Lenox Baker Hospital, N.C. Eye and Ear Hospital, and dozens of specialty medicine clinics, Durham rightly lays claim to title as the nation's City of Medicine.

As Durham made a slow turn from its industrial base, it veered directly into the path of cutting-edge vocations: biotechnology, computers, communications networks, pharmaceutical research. Relying on the combined resources of Duke, UNC, and NCSU, leaders from the state, region, city, and university plunged into creating the 6,800-acre Research Triangle Park, three-quarters of which was in southeastern Durham County. The Park was not an overnight success; for years, the Research Triangle Foundation and research-minded Research Triangle Institute were the only tenants. But when IBM sank footers in a massive 400-acre RTP campus in 1966, the Park's future was assured.

Durham quickly recognized an immediate need for training and industrial education, not only for the new Park employees, but the retraining of its own workforce as it entered the high-tech world of the future. With assistance from the state community college fund, it established Durham Technical Institute (now Durham Technical Community College) near the Park. The school has proven an invaluable asset for the community.

As the Park grew, so did Durham's economy—and population. From 1960 to 1990, Durham County added 70,000 new residents, a 62 percent increase. Projections indicate even larger increases in the future, with a population expected to top a quarter million by the year 2010.

Growth has presented its own set of challenges, but Durham has weathered numerous social, political, and economic storms with the frank, open public discussion that reflects its populace. Got a beef? Call one of the twelve City Council members or the five County Commissioners. Want to speak your peace? Attend one of the many public forums on current issues. Feel the need to disseminate your opinion? Write a letter to the local newspaper, a lively platform for debate. Like to express yourself artistically? Take a class at the Durham Arts Council. Want to expand your mind? Enroll in Continuing Education classes at Duke or Durham Tech. Want to attend law school at night? Apply at North Carolina Central University.

Throughout the variety of opinions, every professional opportunity, all the big-city sophistication and small-city ambience, a single thread pulls Durham together—commitment. Newcomers and natives, students and professors, conservatives and liberals alike care passionately about Durham and its future. They jump into the thick of debate on school issues, water protection, highways—all to Durham's good. Durhamites like to "air" things, and it's the essence of what makes them special.

Today's Durham moves forward at the speed of light, tempered by the wisdom of its history. And it will continue to be molded by its ever-changing population, just as it heeds the whispers of its past. 🖋

🖋 Washington Duke, patriarch of the Duke family, whose generosity, wisdom, and vision shaped the direction, growth, and success of Durham. Courtesy of Duke University Archives.

🖋 Previous page. The Unity Monument was erected on the Bennett farm to commemorate the treaty ending the Civil War for the Carolinas, Georgia, and Florida, which was signed here by Union General William Sherman and Confederate General Joseph Johnston. Photo by Paul Liggitt Photography.

chapter two

THE ECONOMY

The phone rarely stops ringing. It trills during the wee hours of the morning, long before anyone is in the office to answer it, and it continues all day long, spilling into the nights and weekends. The calls come from everywhere: Atlanta to Alaska, across the continent and around the world—as many as 600 a week. And virtually every caller has the same query for the Greater Durham Chamber of Commerce: "What can you tell me about Durham's economy?"

▌Peoples Security Insurance Building overlooks the heart of Durham's vibrant downtown. Photo by Paul Liggitt Photography.

It's an enviable story, even when told in bare-bones, statistical fashion: corporate investment increased by $2.84 *billion* from 1980 to 1993, creating more than 23,000 new jobs. About 140,000 people are employed by Durham firms. The population in Durham and Durham County has grown considerably, jumping 44 percent from the mid-1980s to the mid-1990s. The unemployment rate hovers around four percent, far below what most economists consider full employment. Wages are relatively high, commensurate with the skills needed to participate in Durham's technology-based economy. A family of four generally earns about $40,000. The average three-bedroom home sells for about $115,000. Retail sales are climbing—up 10 percent in 1992 to $1.838 billion a year.

▌ Brightleaf Square is a specialty shopping area, meticulously restored from two elegant brick warehouses. Photos by Paul Liggitt Photography.

The story becomes even more impressive when the stats are fleshed out with real-life examples. Cormetech, Inc., a joint venture between Corning and Mitsubishi, moved into Treyburn Corporate Park in northern Durham County in 1990. In response to higher standards for air and water quality, the company developed sophisticated "scrubbers" that purify emissions from coal-fired power plants. When Cormetech was ready to find a permanent site for its new venture, executives set forth a demanding set of criteria. Durham met every one, according to Tom White, vice president of economic development for the Durham Chamber.

"Cormetech needed productive employees; they can hire bright, talented people from our universities," he said. "They wanted to achieve a high transfer acceptance rate; with our high quality of life, they have little difficulty convincing personnel to relocate here. They required a superior corporate site, and we have multiple parcels available at attractive prices. We also have relatively low construction costs, compared to the rest of the country, so that

firms like Cormetech can get more for their money."

Durham's intellectual climate also met Cormetech's standards. Since the company works closely with governmental regulations, the presence of the Environmental Protection Agency in Research Triangle Park was an exceptional draw. Such scientific partnerships are unique to Durham, and they attract many Fortune 500 firms to the area.

The Stroh Company, famed for its brewery, pursued a new line of scientific research that had potential application in the medical field. To determine whether the concept was sound, Stroh turned to Duke Marine Laboratory scientist Joseph Bonaventura. A collaborative agreement was signed, Apex Bioscience was born, and the partnership launched its research in facilities located just minutes from Duke's laboratories.

Fast-lane innovation is commonplace in Durham, a city accustomed to encouraging the dreams of lucky entrepreneurs. After all, it was here in 1883 that Richard Wright founded a company, originally designed to package tobacco and attach strings to teabags, which ultimately became the Honeywell Electro Corporation. In a plant not far from downtown Durham, Honeywell now manufactures electronic guidance systems for spacecraft and airplanes. It was in Durham in 1910 that an enterprising young pharmacist mixed together a compound now known as B.C. Headache Powders, which is still sold in drugstores nationwide. And in the early days of health insurance, the forerunner of Blue Cross Blue Shield of North Carolina was created for Watts Hospital patients (annual cost of medical insurance for a married couple in 1933: $18). Housed in its landmark "upside-down" glass building, Blue Cross Blue Shield of North Carolina now employs 2,000 workers in Durham and Chapel Hill.

Of course, Durham earned its place in the sun with the emergence of tobacco and textiles in the late 1800s. That lifeline continued to pump money into the local economy well into the middle of this century, setting a standard of steady employment and prosperity. "When I arrived here in 1965, Durham was a rough-and-tumble industrial town," said Chamber President and CEO Robert H. Booth. "Right in the downtown area, we had heavy manufacturing with plants like the Durham Hosiery Mills and American Tobacco. And warehouses that once had tobacco stored in them have now been converted to shops and condominiums. Durham's economy has made the transition from tobacco and textile manufacturing to a high-technology-based economy. Now we are a health care city; we have tremendous technology resources and assets, and we are becoming well known for our biotechnology and pharmaceutical firms," he said. "Although we have decreased our dependence on the tobacco and textile industries, we continue to enjoy huge benefits from their legacy. Duke University, for instance, was created with tobacco money, and today Duke is an incomparable asset for Durham."

▌THE EDUCATION INFLUENCE

Duke University and its companion medical complex, Duke University Medical Center (DUMC), have a profound effect on Durham. These acclaimed institutions are Durham's (and the state's) largest private employers by a wide margin. More than 20,500 workers don a Duke ID badge and go to work in one of hundreds of university offices and labs, located throughout the city and county.

Its sheer size makes Duke University a major player in the Durham economy, by virtue of the thousands of suppliers and vendors that support this "city-within-a-city." Duke generates many of its own products internally, but it often calls on Durham firms to provide everything from food to printing services. Peripheral businesses also benefit through their close proximity to the university. Durham's hotel and motel trade, for instance, greets thousands of visitors and patients who linger a few days at the university or medical center. On graduation weekend at Duke—which coincides with Mother's Day—every one of the 5,000-plus hotel rooms in the city and county are booked —usually a year in advance!

Even Duke cultural events generate business traffic for Durham. The Duke Broadway series attracts crowds from all over the Triangle, the state, and beyond. Since Durham has earned a reputation as the "restaurant capital of North Carolina," out-of-towners make a special effort to dine at one of the city's gourmet eateries before or after a performance.

Durham has become such a coveted place to

▌Signs of downtown renewal are everywhere as evidenced in the Durham Civic Center, adjacent to and part of the Omni Durham Hotel and Convention Center. Photo by Paul Liggitt Photography.

live that countless Duke graduate students who have "lived the good life" here as students choose to stay on, find jobs, and sink roots. They're in good company; as Durham attracts newcomers from every corner of the nation and the world, the local real estate market flourishes, offering a wide variety of home styles and price ranges.

Duke isn't the only educational/economic influence in town. North Carolina Central University (NCCU) enrolls 5,600 students each year and hires about 1,000 faculty and staff members on its Fayetteville Street campus. Like Duke, it depends on local suppliers. Although NCCU, and Durham's other major educational source, North Carolina School of Science and Mathematics (NCSSM), are state-supported, their students pump life into the local economy each school year—at the malls, fast-food outlets, and entertainment. Both schools recently received state funding for multimillion dollar capital improvement programs, sending contractors scrambling to hire local craftsmen to erect the new buildings. Some of those craftsmen learned their trade at Durham Technical Community College, which specializes in vocational training. Durham Tech's brand of voc-ed isn't limited to shop class and secretarial school. Durham Tech offers leading-edge training in robotics, electronics, and computers. Durham Tech courses

▌Duke University's Fuqua School of Business. Photo by Paul Liggitt Photography.

North Carolina Mutual Life Insurance Company was the first, and remains the largest, African-American owned insurance company in the nation. Photo by Paul Liggitt Photography.

Craftsmen hammer out works of art at Vega Metals. Photo by Bob Hopkins/Impact Photography.

Following page. Meridian Business Campus. Photo by Bob Hopkins/Impact Photography.

are so highly regarded among business leaders, the school is sometimes credited with swinging a decision in favor of Durham for relocating companies.

MEDICINE PLAYS AN IMPORTANT ROLE

No one has to "sell" physicians on Durham. They arrive by the thousands! The ratio of physicians to residents is 1 to 79, the third highest in the nation and five times higher than average. Drawn by Duke Medical School, medical research, and clinical opportunities, physicians tend to congregate in Durham's many medical facilities. There are about 1,700 at DUMC; across the street at the Durham Veterans Affairs Medical Center, there are 400 doctors on staff. Durham Regional Hospital has granted more than 400 physicians staff privileges, and there are hundreds of doctors practicing medicine in private clinics, group practices, and the many diet centers located in Durham.

Clearly, medicine makes up a healthy chunk of Durham's economic base. Nurses, physician assistants, laboratory personnel, administrators, scientists, custodians, aides—thousands of people work in health-related professions in Durham. Many of them spend their work days at one of the three major hospitals; others work in smaller specialty hospitals like Lenox Baker and NC Eye and Ear. Still others staff much-needed outpatient clinics, such as Lincoln Community Health Center; or they work for one of the pharmaceutical research companies like Glaxo Wellcome in Research Triangle Park.

RTP IS A CATALYST FOR NEW BUSINESS

Pharmaceutical companies are a highly visible part of Research Triangle Park (RTP), but they're just part of the big picture. From giant IBM (which has 11,000 people cashing "Big Blue" paychecks every month) to tiny Sigma Xi, a scientific research association with 38 employees, RTP is nothing if not diverse. The Park has stayed true to its original purpose—to

provide an idyllic setting for pure research. The largest Durham County portion was subdivided first; the Wake County portion opened its first plant in 1994. Given the tremendous impact of the firms in RTP proper, it's not surprising that hundreds of "just outside the Park" businesses sprang to life. More than 20 satellite, industrial, office, and research parks ring the perimeter of RTP. Some RTP firms lease additional space there; some space is occupied by support companies or small niche research firms.

"We're beginning to see a lot of small entrepreneurial companies starting up to supply the largest companies. That kind of development continues to add an element of newness and excitement to the business climate," said Tom Keller, dean of the Fuqua School of Business at Duke University. *Inc.* magazine recently cited the Raleigh-Durham area as one of the best places in America for business start-ups.

The area is also becoming a strong market for export ventures, thanks to the Triangle World Trade Center. And the Park has energized an international mind-set that smoothes the way for non-U.S.-based companies to establish facilities here. Germany's Freudenberg Nonwovens and Freudenberg Spunweb operate expansive manufacturing plants in northern Durham County. Organon Teknika Corporation from Holland nestles near Cormetech in Treyburn Corporate Park. Mitsubishi Semiconductor America, Inc., headquartered in Japan, churns out semiconductors at its pristine manufacturing facility built amidst the pine trees on Old Oxford Highway. The Japanese version of *Newsweek* has recommended the Triangle as one of the best places in the world to live for Japanese expatriots and their families.

THE HOME-TOWN TEAM THRIVES

Durham's thriving business climate is not solely dependent on relocations and start-ups, however. Durham's long established core businesses have grown strong over the past few decades. Central Carolina Bank, for instance, maintains corporate headquarters in its *art nouveau* building in downtown Durham. A fixture in the financial world, CCB now has 41 branch offices across the Triangle and has expanded even beyond the tri-county area with well-planned acquisitions.

In like fashion, North Carolina Mutual Life Insurance Company was the first, and remains the largest, African-American owned insurance company in the nation. From humble beginnings in Durham's Hayti neighborhood, the company has diversified into the financial market with several subsidiaries. The company employs 150 in its Durham headquarters office alone. Durham also boasts its own African-American owned Commercial Bank and Community Savings Bank.

In its infancy in the 1950s, Durham's Strawbridge Studios shot portraits of schoolchildren. Part of the company broke off to specialize in photo processing as Colorcraft Corporation. Today, operating as Qualex, Inc., the company is still based in Durham, has 7,500 workers nationwide, and is the largest photofinisher in the world. Strawbridge Studios continues its photographic tradition, advertising that it is the "oldest school photographer in the South."

Even local government is a key player in the local marketplace. Durham City operates with an elected body of 12 Council members and a Mayor. The City Manager supervises a $157 million budget. Durham County is governed by an elected board of five County Commissioners with a County Manager who handles operations. The County's budget tops $236 million each year and includes local supplements for Durham Public Schools. Both the City and County carry highly coveted AAA bond ratings, the result of careful fiscal management over the years. Durham City and County governments provide jobs to more than 2,800 citizens; an additional 4,000 teachers, principals, staff, and operations employees are part of the public school system.

There are dozens of success stories in Durham—Duke Power Company, GTE South—the list is far too long to be inclusive. But all of the home-team companies seem to share a single vital characteristic: the ability to envision an even brighter tomorrow for Durham.

Erwin Square is home to many of Durham's "hometown-team" businesses. Photo by Paul Liggitt Photography.

That optimism is what propels Bill Kalkhof through each day. Kalkhof is president of Downtown Durham, Inc., an organization committed to the invigoration of Durham's central city. "In order to have continued economic development, you have to have a vibrant downtown area," says Kalkhof. Signs of renewal are everywhere: in the Durham Convention Center and Omni Durham Hotel, in the new Bull City Business Development Center, in the Peoples Security Insurance Building, and new county offices. A full-fledged arts and entertainment district is being created that will encompass the new Durham Bulls Athletic Park, the Durham Arts Council, the newly refurbished 1920s-style Carolina Theatre, nightclubs, and a clutch of fine restaurants, including those in the Brightleaf Square area. Brightleaf Square is a specialty shopping area, meticulously restored from two elegant brick tobacco warehouses. Brightleaf hosts small boutiques, fine food, street opera, and a devoted shopping clientele.

It's doubtful anyone would ever be in need of a place to shop in Durham. Along almost every main street in Durham, the retail trade thrives—strip malls, clustered stores, and giant malls. Two major malls abut Durham's main highways. South Square Mall is located on Highway 15-501, in close proximity to the I-40 interchange and nearby Chapel Hill; Northgate Mall adjoins Highway 70 and I-85. The busy parking lots at the malls and the array of satel-

RDU International Airport has evolved from a tiny one-runway operation to a major air thoroughfare with carrier service by seven major airlines plus commuters. Photo by Bob Hopkins/Impact Photography.

lite retail outlets are testament to the buying power of this area.

DESTINATION: DURHAM

Don't assume those parking lots are full of *local* vehicles, though. Reyn Bowman, executive director of the Durham Convention and Visitors Bureau, reports that about a third of Durham's three million visitors manage to squeeze in a little shopping and entertainment while they're here. "Conservatively, we estimate visitors spend about $411 million in Durham each year," said Bowman. "The most popular destinations are Duke University, the Museum of Life and Science, and the Durham Bulls baseball games." Visitors usually arrive in Durham by car, but almost one-fifth touch down at the Raleigh-Durham International Airport (RDU).

RDU straddles I-40 and Highway 70, and is located centrally between Durham and Raleigh. The airport has evolved from a tiny one-runway operation to a major air thoroughfare with carrier service by seven major airlines plus commuters. John Brantley, director of the RDU Airport Authority, says the airport mirrors the growth of the Triangle. "The economic health of this region is reflected every day at the airport. Local traffic was up 10 percent in 1994 and cargo was up 18 percent. The airport is the gateway to the region, its prime economic engine," he said.

Durham's robust growth is fueled by a high-octane blend of businesses, professional services, and development. To explore each of them fully would require hours of study. Suffice it to say that without its architects and land planners, its attorneys and accountants, its commercial developers and residential

brokers, its banks and savings and loans, its educators and students, its city and county governments, its artists and craftsmen, its researchers and statisticians, its high tech and low tech, Durham would never have scaled the heights it has reached over the past 150 years. Viewed from every vantage point, Durham's economy is an ever-changing kaleidoscope of activity.

Durham's retail trade thrives! Photo by Bob Hopkins/Impact Photography.

The new Durham Bulls Athletic Park is a vital contributor to Durham's thriving economy and a centerpiece for downtown. Photo by Bob Hopkins/Impact Photography.

chapter three 3

RESEARCH TRIANGLE PARK

First-time visitors usually are puzzled when they arrive at Research Triangle Park (RTP). There are no entrance gates, rows of corporate buildings, or glass and steel high-rises. Instead, there are trees, quiet roadways, a few grassy knolls and...more trees. Planted at well-spaced intervals along the roadways are contemporary signs—the single hint as to the prominence of the Park's nearly invisible tenants: "Glaxo Wellcome," "IBM," "Nortel." And tucked into the evergreen forests are the corporations, agencies, and institutions that ignite the explosive energy of Research Triangle Park.

National Institute of Environmental Health Sciences (NIEHS), one of RTP's two flagship institutions.
Photo by Chip Henderson.

George M. Herbert, first president of Research Triangle Institute. Courtesy of Research Triangle Institute.

It is energy captured in the intense research of thousands of RTP scientists. Each day, they probe the mysteries of gene therapy and biotechnology, the information superhighway and supercomputers, social policy and environmental protection, digital telecommunications, and semiconductors. Even more impressive...they get answers that change the world. It was here that Astroturf© was invented; that AZT, the first drug to fight AIDS, was produced; that two members of the team that identified the breast cancer gene worked; and that three Nobel laureates conducted their work.

There is always an air of quiet anticipation at RTP; the next earth-shattering breakthrough is poised to occur momentarily—in the labs or buildings where 34,000 workers spend their professional days. This exhilarating, somewhat rarefied atmosphere is made possible through unprecedented scientific cooperation between industry and three highly respected doctoral research universities—Duke University in Durham, NC State University in Raleigh, and University of North Carolina at Chapel Hill.

Development in the Park's 6,800 wooded acres is managed by the not-for-profit Research Triangle Foundation. To preserve the integrity of the Park, only institutions focused on research and development are accepted. There are stringent restrictions on land use: buildings occupy only a fraction of the verdant parklands; RTP firms are encouraged to build out, not up—few buildings rise above the level of the tallest trees.

The Park lands span the Durham/Wake county lines, with about 60 percent of the land—as well as the majority of RTP tenants in Durham County and 40 percent in Wake. In the early days, water and sewer lines were extended into the Durham County portion only, thus ensuring development in the "northern" section of the Park first. The smaller Wake County portion began construction for its first tenants in

Research takes on all forms in the labs of RTP. Courtesy City of Medicine.

1994. The Park is a self-taxing district, but pays property taxes to each adjoining county in which its facilities are located. The exponential growth of the region is linked to the success of the Park—and vice versa.

"There are only two reasons why this Park is so successful," said James Roberson, president of Research Triangle Foundation. "First, are the three universities—Duke, UNC, and North Carolina State. The second is the quality of life as reflected by local governments. There are quality residential developments everywhere. You can enjoy any kind of lifestyle you want, and housing at prices that are still affordable. If you ask any manager at a company in the Park what the biggest attraction is, they'll tell you it's the ability to recruit people to this area." Paradoxically, it was the *failure* to attract and keep people in the Triangle that provided the impetus for creation of RTP.

THE VISION

The year was 1955; North Carolina was hemorrhaging from its academic centers. In the cruelest of ironies, economic development leaders watched helplessly as students matriculated at North Carolina's hard-won, nationally acclaimed universities...then slipped across state lines to find higher-paying jobs elsewhere. The seepage was predictable. North Carolina's economy was dominated by agriculture, furniture and textiles; academics had little place in the tobacco barns or cotton mills. And manufacturers—a potent source of new jobs—had little interest in locating technologically oriented plants in the South. Workers wages reflected this syndrome; North Carolina's wage rates were among the lowest in the country.

For Romeo Guest, president of Greensboro's Romeo Guest Associates, an industrial construction company, the situation was intolerable. As a student at the Massachusetts Institute of Technology (MIT), he had witnessed the thriving industrial development that sprang up near the research laboratories of MIT and Harvard University. He envisioned a similar concept for North Carolina: to encourage industrial investment via research generated by three universities—Duke, NC State University, and UNC. Guest went directly to N.C. Governor Luther Hodges with his proposition using the title "North Carolina's Own Research Triangle."

Hodges immediately recognized the potential of Guest's suggestion and established the Research Triangle Committee. After several fitful starts, the committee moved forward with a plan to create a research park midway between all three universities. About 5,000 acres of Durham County and Wake County pinelands were purchased under the direction of Guest, Wachovia Bank President Robert Hanes, and with the financial backing of New York investor Karl Robbins. The investment group, appropriately named the Pinelands Company, officially dubbed the land "Research Triangle Park," and by 1958, RTP was primed for the business of research.

About the time RTP marketing efforts began, the economy slowed and negotiations with three prospective RTP tenants faltered. The Committee experienced a change in leadership. At the urging of Archie K. Davis, Hanes' successor at Wachovia, the committee reorganized and implemented a two pronged, long-term marketing and development endeavor. A not-for-profit entity, the Research Triangle Foundation, was established to manage and market the fledgling RTP. During a whirlwind, three month fund-raiser for the Park, Davis attracted $1.5 million in private and business support statewide. The Foundation then used the money to buy back the land from Pinelands Company and charter the new Research Triangle Institute (RTI). Sometimes referred to as the Triangle's "fourth university," RTI was founded as a not-for-profit contract research organization and was the first tenant of the Park—one of only a handful during those early, uncertain years.

THE REALITY

A young George Herbert, former executive associate director of California's Stanford Research Institute, stood in the middle of a grassy field in RTP, eyes shaded from the bright Carolina sunshine, and made plans— big plans. He envisioned an arena devoted solely to contract research, utilizing the combined talents of the three local major universities. He could imagine buildings on the horizon—lab space for hundreds of scientists and researchers, administrative offices, commons areas.

Then he came back to reality. As RTI's first

president, he had temporary offices eight miles away in Durham. His staff was so tiny, he could have conducted meetings around his own breakfast table. It was a less than auspicious beginning for an institution that would be the genesis of Research Triangle Park.

But in 1959, George Herbert's vision was enough to sustain the small group of loyal RTI staffers who would shape the Institute. Within seven years, the institute had a staff of more than 280, working on 138 different research projects. Seven buildings had emerged from the Carolina clay to house RTI research and development. When he retired in 1989, George Herbert's foresight had guided the Institute through its first 30 years—a considerable accomplishment for a man who was not himself a researcher.

Today, RTI's campus encompasses 565,000 square feet of laboratory and computer space at RTP, plus facilities at project locations around the U.S. and abroad. There are 1,472 employees, 60 percent of whom are professionally trained researchers. Revenues at the Institute have increased every year with projections topping $135 million in the mid 1990s. Such growth is not unexpected, says RTI President R. Thomas Wooten. "What you have in the Park is one of the nation's largest research institutes which has unusual breadth and a mind-

▌ IBM's original workforce of 2,500 employees has mushroomed to more than 10,000. Photo by Peter Damroth.

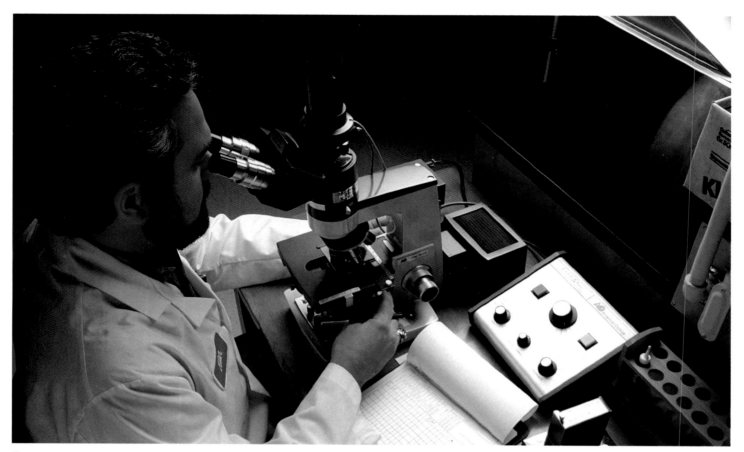

Realization of the dream—lab space for hundreds of scientists and researchers. Photo by Paul Liggitt Photography.

Today, IBM's Research Triangle Park site produces all of IBM's personal computers, including the ThinkPad laptop computer. Courtesy of IBM.

GTE's research in broadband
signal distribution has made the
company one of the founders of
the information superhighway.
Courtesy of GTE.

set to solve problems for industry," said Wooten. "We have the best research staff among any of the research institutes." The Institute specializes in four broad areas of research: public health and medicine, environmental protection, advanced technology, and social policy.

More than any other entity, it was Research Triangle Institute that blazed a trail for the recruitment of other research firms at RTP. The recruitment process meandered along its own cautious timeline, however. In the first five years of RTP's life, only Chemstrand, a division of Monsanto, dared take a chance on the fledgling park, but even it eventually moved away. There was worry, head shaking, and occasional despair over the ambitious project. But in 1965, IBM and the National Institute of Environmental Health Sciences (NIEHS) made landmark decisions by announcing they would build major installations in the Park. The Carolina skies began to clear; Research Triangle Park was finally on the path that would accord it international stature.

The U.S. Environmental Protection Agency's 1,200 staffers help evaluate the health effects of exposure to air pollutants, pesticides, and toxins; they also set standards for air pollution control. Photo by Paul Liggitt Photography.

▮THE SUCCESS STORIES

The two flagship institutions, IBM and NIEHS, a division of the National Institutes of Health, have grown dramatically since the mid-1960s. IBM's original work force of 2,500 employees has mushroomed to more than 10,000. Today, IBM's Research Triangle Park site produces all of IBM's personal computers, including the ThinkPad laptop computer. NIEHS now employs more than 1,000 workers who conduct basic biomedical research on environmentally related diseases. Its stunning lakeside tract was recently augmented by a new 155,000-square-foot structure that houses 250 labs. NIEHS, which also encompasses the National Toxicology Program, has forged closer ties with Duke and UNC medical centers; they will be host sites for NIEHS clinical studies.

Another landmark in RTP, the U.S. Environmental Protection Agency, has °expanded as well with new laboratory and office space. The 1,200 staffers help evaluate the health effects of exposure to air pollutants, pesticides, and toxins; they also set standards for air pollution control.

Rhone Poulenc AG Company, CIBA-GEIGY Biotechnology Research, and BASF Corporation Agricultural Products continue North Carolina's tradition of agriculture, but with a new twist—they conduct trials on plant growth regulators, insecticides, and herbicides that leave old-fashioned farming methods in the dust. Chemicals of another variety occupy the interests of Reichhold Chemicals, Inc., a division of the Japanese firm Dainippon Inks. The company employs 500 workers who conduct research and development for new adhesives, coating resins and polymers for use in a myriad of products manufactured around the world.

Communications is what makes the companies in Research Triangle Park really hum. Nortel produces digital switching systems for the world's offices. About 9,300 employees work for Nortel and Bell Northern Research (BNR), its research and development arm in RTP. Supercomputing is a daily routine at MCNC, a private, not-for-profit corporation that serves as an electronic facilitator of information between the universities and commercial firms. It was also the very first end-user to come on-line on North Carolina's vaunted information superhighway, thanks to GTE South. GTE South provided state-of-the-art digital switches and miles of lightning-fast fiber optic cable in Durham County, including RTP, to bring the superhighway to fruition. The superior communications network in RTP is a strong draw for high-tech companies.

The highest profile among all RTP firms is reserved for pharmaceuticals. When Glaxo, Inc. acquired former competitor Burroughs Wellcome in 1995, it became the largest phar-

Tucked into the evergreen forests of RTP is the U.S. headquarters of Glaxo Wellcome, the largest pharmaceutical firm in the world. Courtesy of Glaxo Wellcome.

maceutical firm in the world. Glaxo Wellcome, with U.S. headquarters in RTP, produces the world's best selling prescription, Zantac (which treats stomach ulcers), developed AZT (the first treatment for AIDS), acyclovir (a landmark drug to fight herpes), Imuran (which prevents organ transplant rejection), and Sudafed (an over-the-counter cold remedy).

THE FUTURE

A small, but worrisome wrinkle in the future of research at RTP is a national disenchantment with long-range projects. "Research, by its definition, is something for the future. We are now defining the future as three years away instead of 20 years away. People who pay the ticket for science are now demanding a return on their investment. We now see research tied to corporate goals," said Thomas Wooten of RTI.

Heightened corporate expectations for research meshes precisely with the mission of the Park, albeit on a tighter timeline. It has held the Park in good stead for 35 years, and will continue to attract new tenants, according to Jim Roberson of the Research Triangle Foundation. "Give us another 20 years and we'll be at maturity," he said. "I think in the future we'll see more of the same kind of interest in the Park—cutting-edge companies who are dependent not on the local economy, but on the world economy. Right now, half of the employees in the Park work for multinational companies. They're here because they represent the strengths of the universities."

chapter four

4 HEALTH

If any of the 2,000 physicians licensed to practice medicine in Durham took the pulse of this vibrant city, he or she would feel its heartbeat quicken at the mere mention of the words "health care."

▐ Durham's progressive medical community is shaped by compassionate, caring, keen minds and modern, world-renowned facilities. Courtesy of Duke Medical Center.

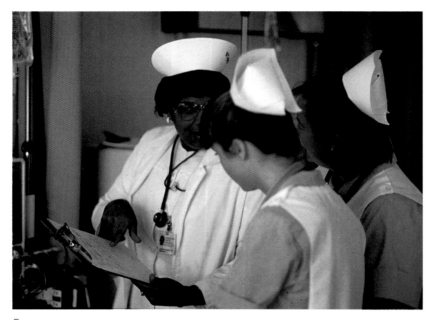

These nurses are part of the efficient and well-trained medical and health care teams that abound in Durham. Photo by Bob Hopkins/Impact Photography.

In a city where one of every three job opportunities is in the health care field, where the quick pace of medical research produces cutting-edge discoveries, where the ratio of physicians to residents is five times the national average, the excitement is understandable. Durham's health focus is multifaceted; not only does it manifest itself in starched emergency room efficiency, it springs from spotless research laboratories and no-nonsense weight-control clinics. The combination of health care resources is so unique that Durham has claimed title as the City of Medicine, an honor bestowed with care and proclaimed with pride.

THE CITY OF MEDICINE

It was Dr. James Davis, a Durham surgeon and former president of the American Medical Association, who first called attention to the growing prominence of medicine in Durham. On an inbound flight to the Raleigh-Durham Airport in the late 1970s, Davis proudly surveyed the panorama of medical facilities sprawled below him: Duke University Medical Center, Durham County Hospital Corporation, Lincoln Community Health Center, the Durham Veterans Affairs Medical Center, and the dozens of health-related corporations and organizations in Research Triangle Park. At that moment, Davis realized that medicine had superseded the dwindling manufacturing trade as Durham's economic lifeline. Davis' insight inspired the

creation of the City of Medicine program, which promotes Durham's medical assets throughout the world.

The program sponsors the prestigious City of Medicine Awards, which recognize outstanding achievement in medical contributions that benefit humankind. City of Medicine annual award winners have been as diverse as newspaper columnist Ann Landers and former U.S. Surgeon General C. Everett Koop. Among the many exceptional scientists are George Hitchings and Gertrude Elion, Nobel laureates in medicine, who developed new techniques for designing drugs that led to a new generation of pharmaceuticals to attack viruses. The two researchers worked together in their Research Triangle Park (RTP) labs.

TOMORROW'S CURES ON THE DRAWING BOARD

Research is an integral and extensive component of Durham's medical and health care enterprise. Literally thousands of workers pore over experiments, sift through data, and draw conclusions in research laboratories across Durham County. Research Triangle Park houses the nation's largest medical research facilities at Glaxo Wellcome Inc. which is also the world's largest pharmaceutical corporation. Pilling Weck has developed innovative surgical

Lincoln Community Health Center serves Durham as an outpatient clinic. Photo by Paul Liggitt Photography.

equipment that encourages less invasive proce-dures from its Durham laboratories. And Durham provides fertile soil for start-up research companies, like Trimeris, Inc., which concentrates on viral diseases such as respira-tory viruses, influenza, hepatitis, and AIDS.

Also hard at work on AIDS research are sci-entists in the Duke University Medical Center (DUMC), which is a designated Center for AIDS Research. AIDS is just one facet of Duke's groundbreaking research. The medical center is world-renowned for its work on cell receptor research and is heavily invested in research on aging, Alzheimer's disease, and human development. Duke is a major cancer research center, and it has made considerable strides in conquering heart disease. In a recent survey of research medical centers, Duke ranked fifth in the nation.

"We conduct almost $300 million in research every year," said Dr. Ralph Snyderman, chan-cellor of Duke University Health System. "We are the seventh-largest recipient of federal funds for biomedical research...The application of that research can be quite profound. Many firms throughout the United States are interested in the Research Triangle because of the opportunity to collaborate with Duke. It has been a strong selling point that one of the

best health care providers in the world is a local hospital for the Research Triangle area."

▌DUKE UNIVERSITY MEDICAL CENTER AND HEALTH SYSTEM

Launched in 1930 with $4 million from the Duke Endowment, Duke University Medical Center and Health System is comprised of Duke University Medical School, the Duke School of Nursing, Duke Hospital, and dozens of Duke research labs. It is also home to Sanus, a managed-care company, and Duke University Affiliated Physicians—both created to meet the challenges of health care reform.

By a wide margin, Duke University Health System is the county's largest employer. More than 13,000 people depend on Duke University Health System for their livelihood; many more thank Duke for their lives. The hospital is con-sidered one of the best in the nation for treat-ment of cancer, AIDS, and heart disease.

Duke is also the county's largest health care provider. With more than 600,000 visits and 30,000 admissions to Duke Hospital annually, the system attracts not only local and regional patients but a worldwide following. "We have people traveling to Duke for medical care from halfway around the world," said Snyderman. "Duke is truly an international hospital."

With 1,124 beds, Duke Hospital is the third-

▌More than 13,000 people depend on Duke University Health System for their livelihood; many more thank Duke for their lives. Courtesy of Durham Convention and Visitors Bureau.

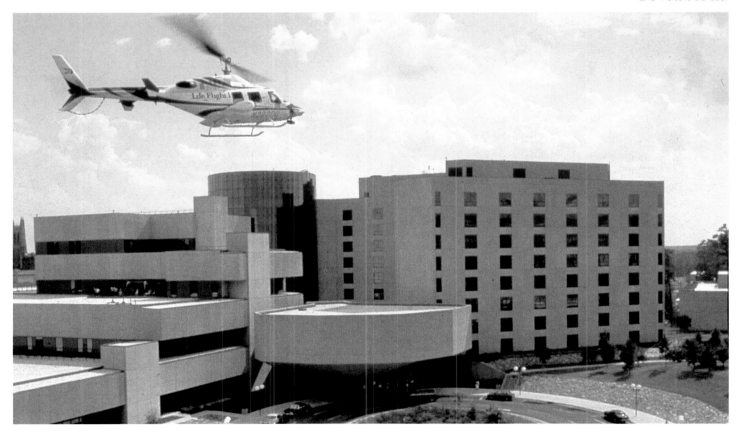

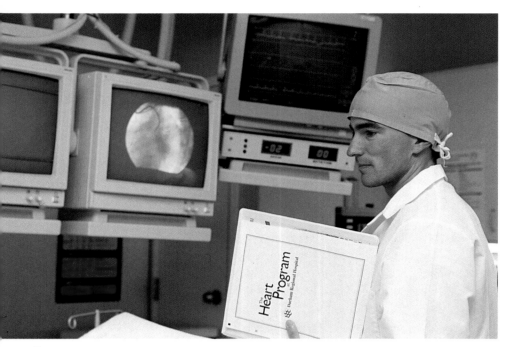

Durham Regional Hospital's heart surgery program ranks among the best in the state. Photo by Bob Hopkins/Impact Photography.

weight babies are born in the first place."

Community health is the bedrock on which the ancestors of the corporation were founded more than 100 years ago. George W. Watts gave Durham its first hospital in 1895; six years later, the Duke family funded a hospital for Durham's African-American community, Lincoln Hospital. After years of separate hospital expansions, the two hospitals consolidated in 1976 to become Durham County General Hospital (now Durham Regional Hospital), a part of the Durham County Hospital Corporation. The Lincoln Hospital site continues to serve Durham as the Lincoln Community Health Center, an outpatient clinic serving Durham's indigent population. Watts Hospital now lives a second life as home to the North Carolina School of Science and Mathematics.

Durham Regional Hospital, located in the exact geographical center of Durham County, is a 451-bed, acute-care facility that serves Durham County plus several adjacent counties. The hospital boasts an impressive lineup of sophisticated medical services and will complete construction of a new Radiation Therapy Center for radiation treatments of cancer in 1996. Built on the Durham Regional campus, the center represents one of the first collaborative efforts between Durham Regional and Duke to provide state-of-the-art health care to the Durham community. In tandem with construction of the Radiation Therapy Center, Durham Regional initiated a multimillion-dollar expansion of the hospital, designed to augment operating room capacity and improve emergency room and outpatient services.

Durham County Hospital Corporation is the umbrella organization for a variety of health care options: Lincoln Community Health Center; the county's Emergency Medical Service, headquartered at Durham Regional; Oakleigh, a substance abuse treatment center; Durham Ambulatory Surgical Center, an outpatient surgery facility; Metropolitan Durham Medical Group, an internal medicine practice; and Watts School of Nursing. Watts School of Nursing, the oldest diploma nursing school in North Carolina, was founded in 1895 with Watts Hospital.

largest teaching hospital in the nation. Highly regarded in the medical education community, Duke University Medical School turns away 60 applicants for each one it accepts. The school and its distinguished faculty consistently rank among the top 10 medical schools in the country.

During the rapid changes in health care that occurred in the mid-1990s, Duke turned its attention to health care reform. In an effort to provide medical care closer to Durham-area citizens, it established Duke University Affiliated Physicians, a network of primary-care practices with Duke physicians on staff. Sanus Corp. Health Systems, a managed-care subsidiary of the New York Life Insurance Company, and Duke have developed a regional managed-care company. The innovative partnership is one of the nation's first alliances between an academic medical center and a for-profit insurance company.

DURHAM COUNTY HOSPITAL CORPORATION

Durham County Hospital Corporation has also responded to changes in the delivery of health care. "The goal is health, not health care," said Richard L. Myers, president of the corporation. "The mission of the Durham County Hospital Corporation is to improve the health status of the community. It's not so much whether you can develop a high-tech system to save low birth weight babies; it's a matter of making a difference in whether low birth

VETERANS AFFAIRS MEDICAL CENTER

Education plays an important role at the Veterans Affairs Medical Center, located just seven miles from Durham Regional's doorstep and across the street from Duke North Hospital. Durham's VA Medical Center welcomes students from a variety of medical programs into its 10-story medical facility.

With a 382-bed, acute-care hospital and a 120-bed, long-term care center, the Durham VA is one of the top five most complex VA medical centers in the country. More than 200,000 veterans from a 29-county area in North Carolina are eligible for treatment at the Durham VA Medical Center (VAMC) of surgical, psychiatric, general, and specialty medical needs. Its Women's Center pays particular attention to the needs of female veterans. And the Extended Care and Rehabilitation Center (ECRC) provides rehabilitation services for veterans who no longer need hospitalization, but who are not yet able to resume an independent life at home.

The Durham VAMC hosts several national VA programs, such as the new National Center for Preventative Health, a program targeted at promoting healthy lifestyles for veterans. Durham is the site for the Regional Medical Education Center, a regional VA training center. Durham's VAMC is also the site of the VA Center for Quality Management Institute.

More than $14 million in VA and National Institute of Health research funding finds its way to the Durham VAMC each year. The Durham facility is ranked fifth in VA research programs among all 171 VA medical centers nationally. VA researchers have won international acclaim for their work on AIDS; every

VA physician has a dual appointment at Duke Hospital.

Former VAMC Director Barbara Small likes to remind visitors that Durham has a rare combination of health care viewpoints. "We are a federal medical installation; Duke is a private medical institution; Durham Regional is a county medical facility; and if you look down the road to Chapel Hill, there is a state medical facility (NC Memorial Hospital, part of the University of North Carolina System) — all within 20 miles! What better place for implementation of health care reform?"

▌*THE DIET CAPITAL OF THE WORLD*

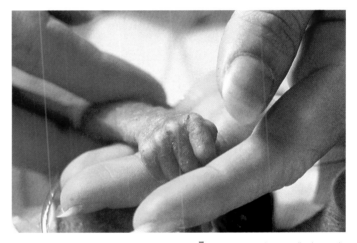

All indicators point to wellness and healthy living as the wave of tomorrow's health care, and Durham is well positioned in this arena. Since the 1930s, more than 25,000 people have visited the famed Rice Diet Center, shedding tons of excess weight. The Rice Diet Clinic provides three meals a day, daily yoga and meditation, education, and group support.

In a slightly different vein, Structure House offers a residential diet program that tackles behavioral changes and the psychological aspects of weight reduction. Structure House

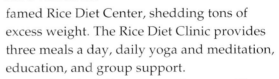

▌ All who receive medical care in Durham find themselves in good hands. Courtesy of Duke University Medical Center.

▌ More than 200,000 veterans from a 29-county area in North Carolina are eligible for treatment at the Durham VA Medical Center. Courtesy of Durham VA Medical Center.

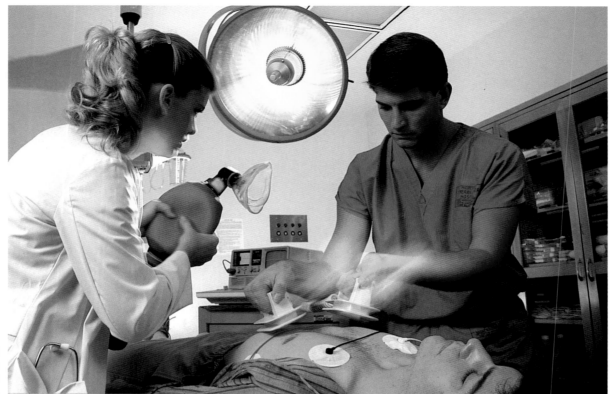

facilities resemble a health spa with its fitness center, indoor and outdoor swimming pools, and private apartments. But the staff takes weight loss seriously, with attention to medical, nutritional, and psychological factors.

The national focus on these and other weight loss centers has earned Durham the unofficial title of "Diet Capital of the World." It is a distinction well deserved, according to Structure House founder Gerard Musante. "With a year-round temperate climate, our friendly, welcoming community, and the cutting-edge medical expertise, Durham is truly a mecca for those who must lose weight," he said.

THE FUTURE HOLDS PROMISE

Medicine and health care form the core of Durham's economic and social base. The hundreds of clinics, specialty hospitals such as NC Eye & Ear Hospital and Lenox Baker Children's Hospital, the patient support networks such as Ronald McDonald House and

Caring House, the diet clinics, and research labs that weave the fabric of Durham's health care tapestry are stepping up to meet tomorrow's health care challenge.

Regardless of the outcome of reform, Durham will remain a leader in medical knowledge, research, and application. The City of Medicine will adapt, change, and flourish, no matter what scenario emerges from the discussion and debate over health care. And its citizens will live healthier, more productive lives thanks to the dazzling spectrum of health care opportunities. *d*

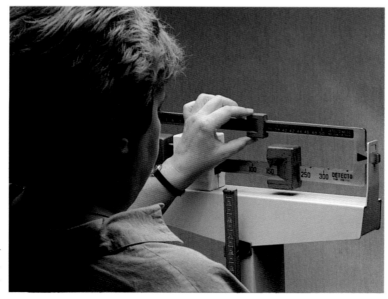

chapter five
EDUCATION

There is an unbreakable ribbon
that weaves itself into the very fabric of life
in Durham, threading its way through
the high school chemistry lab, the corporate
boardroom, the ivory towers of the
universities, and the preschool playground.
It is Durham's passion: education.

Nowhere is the unifying force of education so apparent as in Durham Public Schools.
Photo by Bob Hopkins/Impact Photography.

At some level, education touches every quadrant of Durham: through the public or private schools, the universities, the state residential high school, the community college. But Durham's educational resources refuse to be restricted to classroom learning. They join hands with the community in a strong network of mutual support: university students donate precious free time to Durham's charitable agencies; businesses join "EDUCATION: TOP PRIORITY" to bolster students and their parents; young vocational students divide their time between classes at the high school and community college. In true Durham fashion, citizens are heavily invested in the processes: for any given educational issue, there is an outpouring of public discussion, creating solidarity among citizens who may disagree on the method but are firmly committed to the outcome—premier educational opportunities. Without exception, education forms alliances between even the most divergent of Durham's spheres.

▌DURHAM PUBLIC SCHOOLS

Nowhere is the unifying force of education so apparent as in the public school system— Durham Public Schools. Consolidated into a single school district in 1992, Durham Public Schools enroll 27,500 students in kindergarten through 12th grade. Although support for public education has always been one of Durham's strongest suits, participation reached fever

pitch during student reassignment, when a citizen-driven plan was adopted.

The momentum continues as the system sets its sights on academic excellence. School board meetings overflow with constituents. More than 10,000 parents, children, and interested citizens turned out for the first Magnet Schools Fair. An audit of the school system's day-to-day operations received the voluntary counsel of top local professionals. "The worst emotion is apathy, but there's certainly no apathy about public education in Durham!" declared Dr. C. Owen Phillips, superintendent of Durham Public Schools.

Phillips and an energetic seven-member school board are determined to implement the community's strongest demand: a world-class school system. "We are a cutting-edge school system," said Phillips. "We have made some radical changes and improvements; now we want to make our schools even greater."

En route to that goal, the system established a series of magnet schools, including two year-round elementary schools, a foreign language immersion program, an elementary math and science technology school, a Montessori school, and a new $28 million model high school at Hillside. The former Durham High School is slated to become a centrally located Magnet Center, offering a variety of magnet specialties: visual and performing arts, international studies, and even a corporate-supported technology training center that will prepare students for tomorrow's jobs in Research Triangle Park and beyond. Closer attention to student achievement has produced measurable results: scores on the Scholastic Aptitude Test jumped an unprecedented 14 points in one year, and standardized test levels increased at almost every grade level.

Voters support public education with their tax dollars. The system recently completed a $200 million locally funded capital improvement campaign that added and upgraded schools; the district now boasts 46 state-of-the-art schools plus a hospital school.

As an adjunct to the public school system, the Durham Public Education Network garners financial and volunteer support for the schools and translates it into groundbreaking programs such as the Teacher of the Year Award, Honor Card, endowed chairs in science, and grants for

▌Hillside High School, Durham's new $28 million state-of-the-art model high school. Photo by Paul Liggitt Photography.

public school teachers. As one of the state's largest and most progressive education foundations, the Network also spearheaded a $6 million campaign to benefit staff development, magnet schools, and the Communities in Schools Academy, an alternative school.

Local colleges and universities also extend a helping hand to Durham Public Schools. Duke University, North Carolina Central University (NCCU), and Durham Technical Community College have established partnerships with the schools. Another educational influence—the North Carolina School of Science and Mathematics—breaks new ground with its programs, which often get their "preflight" testing in Durham's public classrooms.

▌*NCSSM*

Laser technology, virtual textbooks on computer CD-ROM, the information superhighway—they're part of the everyday experience at the North Carolina School of Science and Mathematics (NCSSM). "We're trying to stay 10 years ahead of the curve of education," said Dr. John Friedrick, director of NCSSM.

About 550 juniors and seniors spend their last two years of high school in residence on the NCSSM campus. They are the cream of North Carolina's high school crop; only 30 percent of all applicants are accepted into the program, which maintains strict geographical, gender, and racial equity.

Founded in 1982 to encourage interest in science and mathematics across North Carolina, NCSSM has been called "One of the Best Schools in America," "The Best Magnet School in the U.S.," and the "School of Dreams." It has the highest number of National Merit Scholars per capita of any school in the country; it sent two students as part of the five-member U.S. team to the international physics competition in Beijing, China; it is the only high school with two students who earned perfect scores on the Scholastic Aptitude Test in the same year. Clearly, students at NCSSM are challenged by their curriculum.

Friedrick says the school's focus is not on NCSSM students alone, however. "Our kids are all the kids of North Carolina, not just the

▌Founded in 1982 to encourage interest in science and mathematics across North Carolina, NC School of Science and Mathematics has been called, "One of the Best Schools in America," "The Best Magnet School in the U.S.," and the "School of Dreams." Photo by Bob Hopkins/Impact Photography.

residential students," said Friedrick. "We are an R&D site for education, a pacesetter. Our charge is to share our knowledge with the rest of the school systems in the state. We try to provide courses for students across the state that aren't available in the local school system."

That means jumping on North Carolina's information superhighway, a network of fiber optics that can transfer billions of data bits from one end of the state to the other in a matter of seconds. NCSSM takes full advantage of the highway; the school videotapes academic classes in science and humanities, then transmits them electronically to students in remote school systems. "It's called Distance Learning," explains Friedrick. "We can even invite the students to come here to NCSSM, stay in the new Royall Outreach Center for a couple of days, and use our laboratories for experiments that can't be conducted in their home schools." NCSSM plans to increase distance learning course offerings with university-level courses that will permit high school students to earn advanced standing for college.

After graduation, some of NCSSM's student population find a collegiate home at nearby Duke University. Inside its Gothic walls, Duke offers its own brand of fast-access education—with a national reputation.

Durham's passion—education—is evident in the faces of these bright young elementary students. Photo by Bob Hopkins/Impact Photography.

Graduation Day—A proud moment for this university graduate and her father. Photo by Bob Hopkins/Impact Photography.

Numerous volunteer mentoring programs help provide a stable base for learning.
Courtesy of *Herald Sun Newspapers*/Photo by Walt Unks.

State-of-the-art robotics labs at Durham Tech bring students into the 21st century of research and manufacturing.
Photo by Bob Hopkins/Impact Photography.

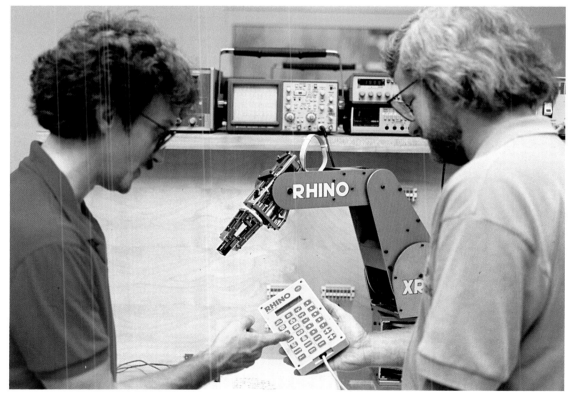

Through a unique visiting scholars program, national and international journalists take mini-sabbaticals at Duke.

Duke's School of Law and the Fuqua School of Business consistently rank among the top 10 in the United States. The Duke University Divinity School, rooted in the Methodist Church, is an acknowledged leader in religious education. And Trinity College, Duke's bastion of liberal arts studies, is exceptionally well known, as is the School of Engineering.

New to the Duke roster is the School of the Environment, one of only three such graduate programs in the United States. "When everyone becomes more concerned about the environment, issues like global warming, coastal erosion, and planetary diseases move to the forefront," said Nannerl O. Keohane, president of the university. "We are a young, creative university—among the nation's best—and we should take advantage of that creative energy to be ahead of the curve, to help solve the world's problems while we continue to offer a very strong academic program."

In addition to their rigorous course schedule, an estimated 85 percent of all Duke students volunteer in Durham's charitable agencies, which range from public schools to the local soup kitchen. Keohane encourages such volunteerism and sets the example by lending her support to vital community projects. "We have the resources to be helpful, particularly in education," she said. "We certainly can't solve all the problems, but we want to do what we can."

Keohane is particularly interested in fostering a reciprocal relationship with the Durham community. Duke invites the public to use the expansive Perkins Library, attend Duke's Broadway series, and take classes at the Duke Institute of Learning in Retirement or Duke Continuing Education. "We want people to feel welcome at Duke," said Keohane. Durham appreciates the sentiment and returns the favor.

❚ DUKE UNIVERSITY

For a young university—James B. Duke endowed the university in 1924—Duke's stature in academic circles is astounding. Despite its southern exposure, it is considered one of the "Ivies," along with its New England counterparts. The university enrolls only 6,100 undergraduates and is highly selective; only one in nine applicants is accepted. Graduate and professional school standards are even higher; just 4,700 grad students are permitted to matriculate at Duke.

The prestigious graduate school programs, which directly impact undergraduate education, attract some of the most astute faculty anywhere in the world. Author Reynolds Price writes and teaches from his Duke office; Dr. Allen Roses conducts his nationally publicized Alzheimer's research at Duke University's renowned medical complex; syndicated columnist William Rasberry teaches in the Terry Sanford Institute of Public Policy.

❚ NORTH CAROLINA CENTRAL UNIVERSITY

In like vein, Durham stands proudly behind the nation's first state-supported liberal arts college for African-Americans: North Carolina Central University (NCCU). The university enrolls 5,600 undergraduate and graduate students on its 104-acre campus, with noted programs in nursing, criminal justice, library and information science, business, and education.

NCCU founder, Dr. James E. Shepard. Courtesy of Durham Convention and Visitors Bureau.

On the horizon is a new emphasis on the environment. Chancellor Julius Chambers convinced lawmakers in the state capital to approve a degree program in environmental science that will complement Duke's new graduate studies in the same arena.

The university has also branched into the brave new world of biomedical technology. Schematic drawings for a biomedical/biotechnology building are under advisement; construction should be complete by the late 1990s. Ambitious expansion plans call for a long-range outlook that may increase the size of the campus to include the old Hillside High School and surrounding area. The university has asked the state for funds to revamp athletic facilities, renovate aging buildings, and add a new Law School and School of Education.

Since 1993, the university has forged stronger bonds with other universities and corporations in the Research Triangle. "I came here complaining about our lack of participation in Research Triangle Park and the Park has responded very favorably to our overtures," said Chambers. "We now have a connection with MCNC and EPA, which is helping us develop our environmental science curriculum. We are also working with Duke, (UNC at) Chapel Hill, and (NC) State. I feel very strongly that soon we will become a four-cornered research area, the Research Square!"

"Central," as it is known to Durham residents, was founded as a training center for African-American ministers and has deep roots in the African-American community nation-

wide. "A narrow focus on minority affairs is an appropriate role for the university," says Chambers. "Major research institutions don't address the interests and needs of minorities, here or nationally. We are working on a way to help fill that void," he said. NCCU's acclaimed Law School specifically addresses the legal issues of minorities; the new biomedical program will look at the effects of medical treatment on minority patients. Despite its proud heritage as a historically black college and university, Central seeks diversity. Currently, the nursing program is racially balanced, and the Law School—the only program that offers a law degree through night classes—is predominantly white. Even more importantly, the university seeks academic equality. "We want to make sure that we are providing competitive education, so that our students measure up to undergraduates everywhere. We want to be the liberal arts undergraduate university for the Triangle," said Chambers.

Durham stands proudly behind the nation's first state-supported liberal arts college for African-Americans: North Carolina Central University. Photo by Paul Liggitt Photography.

Chambers has embarked on a full-fledged, fund-raising campaign to raise the school's endowment and financial footing. Generous donations have been received from Triangle corporations and private citizens. The university gives back to the community through the first-ever state requirement for community service, also instituted by Chambers. The new requirement went into effect in the Fall, 1995, semester, with applause from Durham. NCCU students work in more than 40 Durham agencies.

DURHAM TECH

With more than 20,000 students, most of whom live within a 25-mile radius of the college, Durham Technical Community College is Durham's most accessible (and low-cost) source of higher education. The main campus, located on Lawson Street, houses an impressive library, Continuing Education building, high-tech labs, administrative offices, and classrooms. The new northern satellite campus is strategically placed for population and corporate growth expected in the northern portion of Durham County. Robotics labs, computer labs, and continuing education classes peacefully coexist on the property adjacent to Treyburn Corporate Park and Treyburn residential neighborhoods. There are also smaller satellites in Chapel Hill and Hillsborough. About 110 full-time faculty teach at Durham Tech, plus 375 part-time instructors.

Long touted as a hub for corporate training, Durham Tech also offers a broad variety of educational opportunities for the vocational and technical careers that flourish in Durham. A wide range of business courses are offered, as well as computer and real estate classes. Industrial and engineering technologies courses are as diverse as architectural drafting and automotive mechanics. And Durham Tech provides expert training for Durham's public servants—fire protection, criminal justice, and private security. Continuing Education classes regularly update the skills of law enforcement officers. In keeping with the high profile of health careers, Durham Tech offers an associate's degree in nursing and a dozen other health-related career courses. Students who need to revisit their high school education can earn a GED from Durham Tech, too.

Durham Tech is the home of the two-year associate's degree in arts or science. Each

Durham Technical Community College is Durham's most accessible source of higher education. Photo by Paul Liggitt Photography.

Durham Tech course is designed to meet the exacting standards of the University of North Carolina System. That means students are able to transfer credits to any college or university in the state.

Education in all its forms—through the private sector and public institutions—is part of the life's blood of Durham. Its citizens respect and appreciate its myriad opportunities, as the spark of learning bursts into full flame in the classrooms and research laboratories that stoke the fires of discovery. 🖉

Previous page. A common sight...Duke students studying on the quad. Courtesy of Duke University.

chapter six

PEOPLE & THEIR NEIGHBORHOODS

On an average day, 67 languages are spoken in the Durham Public Schools. Not taught. Spoken. By students and, by necessity, their teachers. This startling statistic is a powerful reminder that Durham is indeed a community of incredible diversity. Turn your attention to the voices at any public gathering and you'll catch snippets of Durham's accents: perhaps the soft twang of Tennessee or the rapid-fire delivery of New Jersey; the slipped syllables of Japan; and always, the familiar inflection of North Carolina's Piedmont. They blend in perfect pitch, creating a rich symphony that reverberates across Durham County.

The children of Durham's neighborhoods are as unique and diverse as the opportunities that abound in this city of discovery. Photo by Paul Liggitt Photography.

Habitat for Humanity volunteer assisting a proud future homeowner to build her own home in Shirley Caesar Court. Courtesy of *Herald Sun Newspapers.* Photo by Bernard Thomas.

Durham's cosmopolitan outlook is unique for a community of almost 200,000 residents. It hearkens to Durham's earliest days when a strong work ethic was the great leveler of race and culture. From the beginning, Durham's multicultural groups lived and worked together in harmony. Ironically, it is "work"—in its corporate and academic form—that continues to propel Durham forward as an international crossroads.

The magnetic presence of Research Triangle Park and similar corporate environs has a tremendous impact on Durham's ethnic composition. Many RTP corporations have international affiliations, which bring multinationals to live in the Triangle. RTP has its own Foreign Trade Zone, encouraging international commerce. Durham's universities and colleges also attract a number of out-of-town, out-of-state, and foreign students and faculty members. And Durham's base population has always been an energetic ethnic mix. This heterogeneity enriches the community—and makes for some interesting discussions in Durham's economic, social, and political arenas.

"Durham's diversity is a tremendous strength," said Tom White, vice president of economic development for the Greater Durham Chamber of Commerce. "You can feel comfortable if you're an electrical engineer from Japan, a scientist from Germany, or a pharmacologist from London. I don't think you can find a better place in the Research Triangle area to feel welcome and accommodated."

Durham receives newcomers with genuine friendliness that transcends polite Southern hospitality. Natives and longtime Durham residents (anyone who has lived here for at least five years!) conduct their business efficiently, without sacrificing life's pleasantries. There's an air of unhurried affability in everyday transactions: grocery clerks smile, receptionists inquire about your family, construction workers say "Good morning," motorists stop to help fix the flat tire of a stranger. Even within Durham's long-established neighborhoods, understanding overrides differences in race, income, education, gender, philosophy, and heritage. Durham truly is a community ahead of the curve. As the faces of the nation slowly turn toward diversity awareness, it is already a reality in Durham.

Given their divergent backgrounds, it is predictable that Durham citizens might disagree on public policy. What is utterly unique to Durham is the candor with which people from all walks of life reveal those opinions. At every opportunity, Durham citizens step forward to present their viewpoint on virtually any local issue: schools, crime, water protection, development. "In other places, you could run a highway through town without much comment; but in Durham, just mentioning the possibility of a highway produces a tremendous reaction from people," said William V. Bell, former chairman of the Durham Board of County Commissioners. Durham's decision makers wisely adhere to an open-door policy, maintaining a direct line of communication with their constituents. It is not unusual for elected officials to respond to voters not only from their offices, but at home, on the street, even in the grocery store! "In Durham, people are accessible," said Bell. "People feel free to call on those people (in power); and we give them a lot of public forums and public meetings to voice their opinions."

The Eno River proves to be an irresistable diversion for these young girls. Photo by Paul Liggitt Photography.

Several independent political organizations spur public debate: the Durham Voters' Alliance, the Durham Committee on the Affairs of Black People, the People's Alliance, and the Friends of Durham. Even the Greater Durham Chamber of Commerce is known to take a stand on issues that influence the growth of the community. But politics are set aside when Durham's groups unite for a greater good.

When a struggling child masters a reading lesson or an elderly man's face alights as his lunch is delivered, chances are good there's a Durham volunteer involved. Durham volunteers perform the most necessary support services: rocking fitful babies to sleep in hospital nurseries, flipping pancakes to raise money for charity, preparing holiday dinners for the homeless. The depth and breadth of Durham's commitment to its own community is extraordinary. For every cause, there are hundreds who rally in its support, often through a strong network of civic and service clubs. No one

appreciates this commitment more than Beth Maxwell, executive director of the Volunteer Center of Durham, which coordinates volunteer placement. "Durham's volunteers fill vital needs in the community," she said. "Fortunately, we have a strong corps of dedicated people who are eager to donate their time and energy to help others."

In an exemplary project, dozens of Durham's citizens offered to help clean up North Central Durham, a 96-block area targeted for renewal. In one day, the volunteers picked up 279 tons of trash from the streets and yards, earning them a cover story on *USA Weekend* magazine. The cleanup, spearheaded by the Volunteer Center, was named one of ten winners in the magazine's 1995 "Make A Difference Day" effort. The Volunteer Center used the $2,000 grant award to buy playground equipment for the North Central Durham area.

North Central Durham is just one of many neighborhoods that welcomes Durham residents home each day. They are as varied as the people who live there. Durham encompasses lush suburban golf course communities and quiet, tree-lined city neighborhoods; planned communities with playgrounds and parks and apartment complexes with swimming pools and community centers. They proudly wear names like Treyburn, Trinity Park, Woodcroft, Hope Valley, Parkwood, Croasdaile, and Emory Woods and sport an ambience all their own. Neighborhood associations thrive across the county—from Old North Durham to Heather Glen. And even neighborhoods that are more loosely organized congregate in common areas— Edgemont Community Center, for instance.

The spectrum of housing styles in Durham is astonishing. Downtown you can still find magnificent mansions that hint at Durham's former tobacco aristocracy and ornate brick tobacco warehouses

▌ Durham boasts lush suburban golf courses along with a year-round climate for golfers. Photo by Paul Liggitt Photography.

▌ Traditional Southern houses are treasured by many Durham residents. Photo by Bob Hopkins/Impact Photography.

converted to high-style condominiums. Widen the circle a bit and you'll encounter contemporary deck homes favored in Duke Forest and traditional Southern houses found in Forest Hills. Brick is a favorite exterior material, but cedar and stucco make regular appearances. Some Northern transplants are surprised to find that basements, and to a lesser extent garages, are options most Durham homes do without. Usually, however, new residents are pleased with the reasonable cost of housing in Durham.

Overall, housing prices in Durham are among the lowest in the Triangle. In the mid-1990s, the average price for a Durham home was about $115,000, but prices range from the low $60,000s to multimillion-dollar estates. There is a plentiful supply of homes and upscale apartments, thanks to aggressive construction efforts by local contractors. Single-family dwellings are often sited on a good-sized tract of land—one-acre wooded lots are not unusual. And Durham County residences are found in a variety of settings that range from small farms to cluster homes.

■ THE PEOPLE

No matter what part of the county they call "home," many of Durham's citizens regularly find their way to one of the many houses of worship. It is no surprise to find that Durham's religious community reflects the diversity of its people. The predominant denomination in Durham is Baptist in all its forms: American

■ Gracious living along the fairways of Durham's golf course communities is a major attraction for many families. Courtesy of Treyburn.

Baptist, Free Will Baptist, Southern Baptist, and Reformed Baptist. And virtually every religious group on earth is represented in Durham—Methodist, Presbyterian, Catholic, Episcopalian, Pentecostal, Moravian, Mennonite, Lutheran, Greek Orthodox, Jewish, Islamic, Buddhist, Apostolic, and Unitarian Universalist among them.

If Durham's assets were ranked in order of importance, its people would top the list. The mailman who coaches baseball, the business owner who presides over her civic club, the university student who mentors a young child, the government official who spends every evening on the phone with citizens—they all exemplify the quiet strength of Durham's diverse population. As Durham continues to grow, its people will play the starring roles in creating a solid future for the community—a community enriched by the choir of a thousand different accents with a thousand different histories and a thousand different tomorrows. ◩

chapter seven
THE ARTS
7

L*ithe young dancers stream across the stage, a shower of pulsating color. The music grows intense; muscular bodies arch into fluid shapes before an audience that overflows Page Auditorium. Suddenly, the music ends, darkness befalls the performance hall, and thundering applause shakes even the second balcony. This is the essence of the American Dance Festival, the nation's premier modern dance festival.*

The American Dance Festival draws an international crowd of professional dance troupes and dance enthusiasts to the Duke University campus each summer. International Choreographers' performance of *Concrete Forest*. Photo by Rebecca Lesher.

The Festival is a Durham tradition, having been wooed to Duke from its Connecticut roost in 1978. It draws an international crowd of professional dance troupes and dance enthusiasts to the Duke University campus, where for six and a half weeks each summer the stages are alive with contemporary interpretations by today's dance masters and emerging talent.

The American Dance Festival (ADF) presents dozens of exquisite dance performances, but its real gift to Durham is an invitation to "come join the dance." ADF dance classes—for the dedicated dancer and the aspiring wanna-be—are open to anyone who qualifies.

ADF's programs include performances, national and international services, humanities projects, community outreach, educational programs and classes, preservation efforts, and archival and media projects. The world is ADF's stage: in 1995, the Festival offered 42 performances from more than 20 companies. There were three U.S. premiers and 11 world premiers. Locally, ADF contributes to Durham's arts with public panel discussions, local dance demonstrations and community classes.

As the most highly publicized of Durham's artistic endeavors, ADF is a shimmering reflection of the roll-up-your-sleeves-and-participate attitude with which Durham regards its entire arts community. Count on Durham to build sets and sing opera, collect tickets and shape clay, write news releases and open galleries. All the while,

it welcomes with equal appreciation the pre-Broadway debuts of playwright Neil Simon, the quiet majesty of the Ciompi Quartet, and the spirited beat of the African-American Dance Ensemble.

Founded by Chuck Davis in 1983, the African-American Dance Ensemble is a perfect example of art brought directly from the people, to the people. "I realized long ago that the heritage of the African people was disappearing from the American consciousness. I wanted to keep the native dance alive, to introduce people to its strength, and show our youngsters that we have our own heritage." said Davis. Garbed in their colorful African-inspired costumes, Davis' professional ensemble tours the nation 12 months a year, but manages to squeeze in several exuberant performances in Durham. At the end of informal performances, Davis often invites the audience onstage to share in his foot-stomping joy, accompanied by the steady, native drum beat.

African-American art is also the principal thrust of the Hayti Heritage Center, run by St. Joseph's Historic Foundation. The center is a hub of activity for the music, dance, and theater of African-American artists. The center contains the Lyda Merrick Gallery, which exhibits paintings and sculptures by African-American artists. The NCCU Art Museum is located nearby on the campus of North Carolina Central University. Central's art exhibits range from collections of African-American art to works by local artists.

In the Durham Arts Council Building, the Central Carolina Bank Gallery, the Allenton Gallery, and the Semans Gallery offer an ever-changing procession of new artistic talent, including solo exhibits and a prestigious annual juried show presented by the Durham Art Guild. Artists also exhibit at the Duke University Museum of Art and in several small privately owned galleries in the vicinity of East Campus. Durham is fertile ground for aspiring painters, sculptors, potters, actors, photographers, writers, dancers, weavers, and other artists, who find the community nurturing of the delicate chord of creativity.

❚ A LITTLE ART HISTORY

It was in the days of tobacco that Durham began its love affair with the arts. The ornate Academy of Music was built in 1904; when the

❚ CenterFest booths display everything from watercolors to metal works. Photo by Paul Liggitt Photography.

❚ The Carolina Theatre, the grand dame of Durham culture, was restored to her original splendor in 1994. Photo by Paul Liggitt Photography.

building was razed to make way for a new luxury hotel, Durham mourned. The "smell of the greasepaint and roar of the crowd" called again, however; in 1926, the Durham Auditorium was built, the precursor to today's Carolina Theatre. Once the venue for well-rouged show girls and traveling shows, the Durham Auditorium even presented a young Katherine Hepburn who starred here in a touring company of *The Philadelphia Story*. Over the years, the Carolina became a movie house and eventually was closed. Not until 1978, when it was rescued from the wrecking ball by local preservationists, did the Carolina begin its second rise to glory. The grand dame of Durham culture was restored to her original splendor in 1994, and now the arts/movie/video complex is a pivot point for the Durham arts community.

The Durham Arts Council, now housed in the Royall Center for the Arts (the former City Hall), boasts two stages, three art galleries, and classroom facilities for dance, photography, painting, sculpture, weaving, and more. The Arts Council Building is also the home base for a collection of arts groups funded by the Arts Council: the Durham Savoyards, the Durham Art Guild, African-American Dance Ensemble, Young People's Performing Company, Durham Symphony, the Durham Theatre Guild, Triangle Opera Theater, Mallarme Chamber Players, Durham Civic Choral Society, the Durham Chorale, and Carolina Wren Press.

Under the energetic leadership of Executive Director E'Vonne Coleman, the Durham Arts Council celebrated its 40th anniversary in 1994. "Durham has one of the strongest arts communities in North Carolina," she said. "Through the Arts Council, we offer an opportunity for artists to express their talents and for spectators to gain new appreciation of all art forms—from dance to oil painting."

Each September, the Durham Arts Council also sponsors CenterFest, Durham's annual street arts festival (the oldest continuous-running street arts fair in North Carolina). This two-day extravaganza of motion, music, arts, and food attracts more than 80,000 people to downtown Durham. Bands play continuously on three stages; booths display everything from watercolors to metal works; and the smell of ethnic foods mingling in the

Storytime at Hayti Heritage Center. Courtesy of Hayti Heritage Center.

fall air is irresistible.

Lots of CenterFest visitors make it a point to visit The Scrap Exchange booth to create artwork from the colorful scraps of plastic, foam, paper, fabric, foil, and wood. Transplanted here from a national program in Australia, The Scrap Exchange pairs ecological preservation with artistic creativity. Scrap Exchange staffers collect clean, nonrecyclable industrial castoffs and offer them by the bagful to children, parents, senior citizens, teachers, day-care operators—anyone who will allow their imaginations to run wild with "junk art."

DIG THOSE DURHAM BLUES!

Back in the 1930s, some very impressive musicians—Duke Ellington, Eubie Blake, and Benny Goodman—played and lived the blues on the streets outside Durham's fragrant tobacco warehouses. They were the inspiration for a distinctive strain of the blues, known as the "Durham Blues" or the "Piedmont Blues." Today, the Bull Durham Blues Festival honors the early ancestors of this riveting, ragtime art form that features a washboard and harmonica. Durham has been the springboard for contemporary vocalists as well. Famed gospel singer Shirley Caesar won a Grammy for her rich renditions. Nnenna Freelon, a rising star in the world of jazz, recorded her first album in 1991, which was nominated for a Grammy. Four

Today, the Bull Durham Blues Festival honors the early ancestors of this riveting, ragtime art. Photo by Paul Liggitt Photography.

▌Triangle Opera Theatre's production of "Carmen." Photo by Paul Liggitt Photography.

▌The Durham Arts Council offers painting classes for all interested in discovering or developing their talent. Photo by Paul Liggitt Photography.

▌Duke Strings School. Duke University hosts an astonishing number of concerts. Photo by Paul Liggitt Photography.

The Royall Center for the Arts is home to the Durham Arts Council. Photo by Paul Liggitt Photography.

years later, she won the Billie Holliday Award (the artist to whom she is often compared) and the Eubie Blake Award.

Local songsters fill the stages at the Festival for the Eno every July Fourth holiday. Musical styles from bluegrass to jazz waft across the grounds of West Point on the Eno, a park that is the centerpiece of green space flanking the narrow Eno River. The festival also attracts the work of artisans and craftspeople who rent booths to sell their artwork and wares. A new series of concerts in downtown Durham draws crowds to the "Durham Alive!" locations.

Music takes on a more sedate tone at concerts by the Durham Symphony, the Duke Symphony, the NC Jazz Ensemble, St. Stephens Chamber Orchestra, and world-famous violinist Nicholas Kitchen, a Durham native. Duke hosts an astonishing number of concerts and performances, including the North Carolina International Jazz Festival and the North Carolina Symphony. Duke's magnificent Flentrop organs, housed in the Duke Chapel, provide the musical backdrop for the performance of Handel's *Messiah*, a tradition eagerly anticipated each Christmas season since 1933.

DURHAM'S DRAMATIC LIFE

Duke Chapel also served as the location for one of many movies filmed in Durham, *The Handmaid's Tale*. Durham earned its Hollywood star with release of *Brainstorm*, a 1981 thriller filmed in Research Triangle Park. But it was producer Thom Mount, a Durham native, who put Durham on the movie map with his 1987 blockbuster film, *Bull Durham*. The film, which starred Kevin Costner and

Susan Sarandon, loosely chronicled Durham's own minor league baseball team, the Durham Bulls, and featured not only footage of familiar downtown Durham sights, but hundreds of Durham citizens as "extras."

Durham's written words have found their way to film, too. Frances Patton wrote her novel *Good Morning, Miss Dove* in 1954; it soon became a much-loved film by the same name. Durham author Clyde Edgerton, who pens dead-aim North Carolina fiction, has also adapted one of his books for the stage, *Walking Across Egypt*.

The theatrical stages in Durham ring with the impassioned speeches of their actors— famous or not—year-round. Duke's Broadway series attracts a stream of well-known names and faces to the Page Auditorium stage. It was here that the world first witnessed the acting debut of former ballet superstar Mikhail Baryshnikov—as a cockroach! Duke's Institute of the Arts has stepped outside the university to work with community artists and organizations. Diverse companies, such as Manbites Dog Theatre Co. and the Archipelago Theatre, offer performances on a regular basis. And the drama department at North Carolina Central University presents several high-quality productions each year.

Triangle Dinner Theater in Research Triangle Park offers yet another dramatic and dining experience, with dinner theater in the round. And the offbeat Transactors Improv Company tours nationally 11 months a year with its comedy theater, based entirely on audience suggestions. The company has been invited back an unprecedented five times to Charleston, South Carolina's famed Spoleto Festival.

Clearly, Durham's arts community flourishes under the nurturance of its dedicated supporters. With a cultural history that spans its entire life, Durham's outlook on the arts for tomorrow is even stronger than today.

Following page. The colorful Kwanza Festival, the African celebration of Christmas, is held each year during the holiday season. Photo by Paul Liggitt Photography.

chapter eight
8 SPORTS

Once a year, sometime in the middle of March, a curious epidemic spreads across Durham. The affliction, which visits virtually every household, is characterized by a sharp rise in blood pressure, particularly during Atlantic Coast Conference (ACC) basketball tournament games. Symptoms include frenzied excitement throughout the NCAA basketball championships and erratic mood swings that range from ecstasy to despair, often triggered by the final buzzer. To date, none of Durham's prestigious medical clinics have developed a cure for this recurrent ailment. "March Madness" must simply run its course, until the next bout hits a year later.

d

NBA star Grant Hill playing basketball for Duke under Coach Krzyzewski. Photo by Bob Donnan Photography.

LIFE IN THE ACC LANE

Despite the infiltration of Carolina and NC State fans, Duke is the hometown team in Durham. With back-to-back NCAA championships behind them (1991-1992) and a 7-for-10 record in Final Four appearances, the Duke Blue Devils hold a special place in the hearts of their adoring public. Duke players are legendary for their academic as well as athletic prowess; the program has a 97 percent graduation rate, one of the highest in the nation. And the competitive spirit that spurs the team to victory is tempered by the strong sense of ethics imparted by Coach Mike Krzyzewski.

Immediately dubbed "Coach K" by fans who tripped on the pronunciation (and spelling) of his name, Krzyzewski took the reins as head coach of the Blue Devils in 1981. Universally respected, Krzyzewski was named "National Coach of the Year" four times in six years. *The Sporting News* dubbed him "Sportsman of the Year," the first university coach to be so honored. In describing Coach K, the magazine reported: "He's what's right about sports."

If Krzyzewski is what's right about sports, Duke fans are what's right about enthusiastic support. Every home game at Duke is a rare treat, thanks to the antics of the "Cameron Crazies." Their clever, but relentless chants and eye-popping "waves" from Duke's bleacher section have baffled more than one visiting team, giving new meaning to the phrase "home court advantage." Who knows what effect the "Crazies" had on the NBA careers of former Duke stars like Grant Hill and Bobby Hurley?

Another NBA star was Durham born and bred: John Lucas, Jr., coach of the Philadelphia 76ers. Lucas' athletic prowess came to light when he hit the court at Hillside High School in Durham. He played on the ACC circuit (even against Duke!) during his college years at the University of Maryland, then was drafted by the NBA before turning his attention to coaching.

Of course, basketball isn't the only game on campus. The Duke women's soccer team won the NCAA championship in 1993, and tailgating at Duke football games is a Durham tradition. Head football coach Fred Goldsmith, who was named national "Coach of the Year" in 1994, led his team to a berth in the Hall of

Universally respected, Coach Mike Krzyzewski—Coach K—was named "National Coach of the Year" four times in six years. Courtesy of Duke University.

In a region where college basketball is monitored as closely as the stock market and even families argue over Associated Press rankings, March marks the apogee of sports in Durham. It is a month of ACC and NCAA action that breeds the highest hopes and deepest disappointments. Although the thrill of Durham Bulls baseball arrives with fanfare each spring and golf tournaments are held around the calendar, it is basketball that transforms Durham's team loyalty into something akin to obsession.

▌Photo by Paul Liggitt Photography.

▌Courtesy of NCCU/Photo Dietrich Morrison, NCCU.

▌Photo by Paul Liggitt Photography.

▌College sports take center stage each fall as the Duke Blue Devils and the NCCU Eagles take the field.

the top in 1989, when it won the NCAA Division II basketball championship. But it is track and field that puts NCCU on the international athletic map—thanks to the vision of a running coach named Walker.

❙ WALK, RUN, RACE

As head track coach of NCCU, Dr. LeRoy Walker, Jr. helped 89 athletes achieve All-American status and spurred his teams to win 11 Olympic medals in track and field. In 1971, he orchestrated the first exchange between the United States and Africa in the Pan Africa Games, held in Durham even today. As a master motivator, he coached the U.S. track and field team at the 1976 Montreal Olympics; served as chairman of the 1987 U.S. Olympic Festival, hosted by the Triangle; and in 1993, he was named president of the U.S. Olympic Committee. As part of his four-year term, Walker was charged with oversight of the 1996 Summer Olympics to be held in Atlanta, Georgia, the first Summer Olympics hosted by the United States since 1984.

Dr. Walker also serves as honorary chairman of the Fitness Festival for the Duke Children's Classic. Since 1973, celebrities from Hollywood and the sports world have visited Durham on Children's Classic weekend. Like singer Perry Como who has headlined the classic since 1974, the celebs donate their time and talent to raise money for pediatric programs at Duke Hospital. The original Classic kicked off with a golf tournament. Tennis joined the fold a few years later; and in 1986, the Classic Fitness Festival became a fixture, with health walks and competitive races.

Golf is a fanatical experience in Durham. The mild climate lends itself to play 365 days a year, and Durham provides a broad spectrum of courses on which to wield the irons and woods. Croasdaile, Hope Valley, Treyburn, and Willowhaven are private courses with varying degrees of difficulty. There are plenty of public courses, too, including the Robert Trent Jones course at Duke University, accessible through the Washington Duke Inn. Other public courses include Hillandale, Lakewinds, and Lakeshore; and there are driving ranges scattered throughout the community. Dozens of golf tourneys, clinics, and lessons find a way to these and other Triangle courses, making Durham truly a golfer's paradise!

❙ Dr. LeRoy Walker, Jr., former NCCU track coach and the current president of the U.S. Olympic Committee. Courtesy of the USOC.

❙ The Bulls in action in the new $16 million Durham Bulls Athletic Park, considered by some to be the best minor league park in the country. Photo by Bob Hopkins/Impact Photography.

Fame Bowl. Duke is one of the few universities that has been invited to the kickoff in all four major bowls—Sugar, Cotton, Orange, and Rose. In 1942, Duke became the only university outside of California to host the Rose Bowl. Duke lost the WWII era game to Oregon at Wallace Wade Stadium.

Football at North Carolina Central University (NCCU) also attracts a crowd at O'Kelly-Riddick Stadium on the Fayetteville Street campus. The Eagles earned a slot in the 1990 NCAA quarterfinals before returning home. The NCCU basketball team went over

MAKING IT TO THE SHOW

The sod is always greener, however, on the infield at Durham Bulls Athletic Park downtown. Built as a replacement for the old Durham Athletic Park (DAP), the $16 million "D-BAP," as it is sometimes called, is hailed as a minor league miracle. "This is the best minor league park in the country," said Mike Hill, vice president and general counsel to the Bulls. The ballpark was engineered to replicate the nostalgic tone of the DAP while increasing capacity and updating important conveniences (like bathrooms—the new park contains more than 100!).

The 9,033-seat ballpark has a playground for children; superb lawn seating; picnic areas; concessions that include ballpark staples like hot dogs, peanuts, and Crackerjacks plus some newer fare such as cappuccino; and the famous mechanical Durham Bull that snorts and smokes with every home run. It also has the most devoted minor league baseball fans anywhere in the United States! Even before Hollywood producer (and Durham native) Thom Mount immortalized the Bulls in the 1987 hit movie *Bull Durham*, fans overflowed the stadium during every home stand. Bulls' games are one of Durham's finest family outings; friends meet under the canopy, kids get autographs from the players, and several prospective bridegrooms "pop the question" via the lighted scoreboard during a seventh-

inning stretch! One Durham Bulls player even married his sweetheart on the pitcher's mound, running back to the dugout to finish the game under an arch of baseball bats!

The Bulls have been a perennial favorite since the first pitch at the first El Toro Stadium back in 1926. That year, the Bulls brought home the Piedmont League pennant. In 1941, 5,000 El Toro spectators got a taste of major league action when Joe DiMaggio and Peewee Reese faced off in a spring training exhibition game between the Dodgers and the Yankees. Over the years, the Bulls have been affiliated with the Detroit Tigers, the Houston Astros, the New York Mets, and finally, the Atlanta Braves. The Braves have invited several former Bulls players up to "The Show"—Brett Butler, Dave Justice, and Steve Avery among them. With a little help from mascot Wool E. Bull and the eager Bulls audience, almost any player feels like a major leaguer at the D-BAP.

Durham has its share of aspiring baseball players, who start out in Durham's Little League, move up through the neighborhood athletic associations, and eventually play for their high schools. Only a few make it to the minors; the rest are content to frequent Durham's summer recreational leagues. Both men's and women's leagues play in locations across the county. Durham is also noted for its extensive soccer and football leagues for children, plus nationally

Durham provides a broad spectrum of courses on which to wield the irons and woods. Photo by Paul Liggitt Photography.

Durham has its share of aspiring baseball players in the ranks of Little League. Photo by Paul Liggitt Photography.

known sports camps offered at Duke. Lots of folks take pride in the accomplishments of the Northern High School Knights football team, which lost only one game in two years and swept the state championships in 1994.

The amateur athlete finds plenty to do in Durham—boating and water-skiing on Falls Lake, fishing in Lake Michie, tennis at dozens of city parks dotted throughout the town. And it's not unusual to see horseback riders loping through the quiet forests of north Durham. North Durham is also the home of Crystal Downs, which features polo matches every fall. Competitive bicycling comes to life at the Wellspring Criterium, held in the spring; and the City of Medicine is well-known for its races, including the City of Medicine Run in May. Even jump rope skipping reaches new

heights with the Bouncing Bulldogs, an award-winning jump rope team. For sedate sports, there's carrom, a version of Asian finger billiards, which maintains national headquarters in Durham.

Whether it's hiking along the Eno River, swimming in a public or private pool, shooting skeet, or sweating off the pounds in a neighborhood spa, there's never a lack of things to do—aerobically speaking. Any season is sports season in Durham!

Competitive bicycling comes to life at the Wellspring Criterium held each spring. Photo by Paul Liggitt Photography.

chapter nine
CityScapes

It was heady escapism in its day: a lake for swimming, a roller skating rink, dance pavilion, merry-go-round, and a rustic stage that attracted a variety of summer stock performances, accessible via the best ride of them all—Durham's open-air trolleys. Lakewood Park, Durham's first amusement park, opened in 1902 as an enticement to Durham citizens to leave the summer heat of the city behind and travel to the end of the trolley line. In time, trolleys gave way to vintage automobiles, the lake was filled in, and a shopping center was erected. Today, the splash of swimming in Lakewood is heard only in the YMCA's indoor pool. But Durham hasn't lost its lust for entertainment; there are dozens of attractions across the county.

West Point on the Eno features a working gristmill, blacksmith shop, and photography museum. Photo by Paul Liggitt Photography.

■ The chinese wisteria covering the pergola in the Sarah P. Duke Memorial Gardens grows more beautiful with the passage of time. Photo by Paul Liggitt Photography.

▌THE STATE OF HANDS-ON SCIENCE

It lacks a merry-go-round and has yet to announce plans for a dance pavilion, but the Museum of Life and Science is undoubtedly Durham's most visited exposition. The highly interactive museum is nationally known for its innovative exhibits that graphically illustrate the principles of science. Children pump "blood" through a network of vessels to emulate the human circulatory system; families can create their own miniature 13-foot tornado; adults are fascinated by the museum's aerospace display; and the WaterPlay exhibit in Loblolly Park grants permission to the very young and the very young-at-heart to behave like children!

The 70-acre museum site contains one of the largest collections of native wildlife in the state. In the indoor Carolina Wildlife area, there is an aviary, a butterfly house, a water playground for otters, and dozens of small animal exhibits. Outside, farm animals greet visitors en route to the Ellerbee Creek Railway, which tours the museum's large animal exhibit of bears and wolves. By the turn of the century, the museum plans a tenfold increase in outdoor exhibit space, which will add a dramatic conservatory with tropical plants and living butterflies and herald the return of the museum's life-sized dinosaur replicas.

The most engaging part of the museum is its emphasis on hands-on learning. Every visitor is encouraged to touch, manipulate, question, and experiment. "People learn best what they almost already know," said Tom Krakauer, executive director of the museum. "The exhibits we have give visitors of all ages and backgrounds the chance to experience science for themselves." Krakauer's approach is a catalyst to learning for hundreds of teachers and their students, who arrive at the museum by the school busloads. They make up fully one-third of the museum's 300,000-plus visitors each year, arriving from 62 North Carolina counties.

▌DURHAM'S GREAT OUTDOORS

The Sarah P. Duke Memorial Gardens attract Durham visitors and residents alike daily to peruse the breathtaking horticultural displays. The Gardens bloom three seasons a year with spring bulbs, summer annuals, and fall chrysanthemums plus an everchanging display of perennials.

Originally constructed in 1935 with a $20,000 gift from Sarah Duke, the widow of Benjamin Duke, the first gardens were plagued by washouts from an unruly creek that flooded its banks after every hard rain. After Sarah Duke died in 1936, her daughter, Mary Duke Biddle, was persuaded to finance a much-improved (and relocated!) garden in honor of her mother. The Italian-influenced gardens opened in 1939 with terraces planted with flowers, flagstone steps leading to a circular pergola covered with Chinese wisteria, and a pool at the bottom of the ravine, flanked by a limestone rock garden. Duke Gardens has grown even more beautiful with the passage of time. A formal rose garden was planted; an impressive entry gate and parking lot were developed on Anderson Street; a quiet garden of native North Carolina plants was established deep in the 55-acre tract; and an open-sky garden and an adjacent lake solved the persistent flooding problems.

Some visitors seek meditation and solace in the gardens; others frolic on the lush lawns; many have spoken their nuptial vows here; still others make a serious study of the specimens. Duke Gardens welcome them all with open arms 365 days a year—rain, shine, or snow. It is an embrace Duke is proud to offer and Durham is fortunate to receive.

The Gardens are just one of the natural gifts Duke shares with its community. Duke Forest spans 7,700 acres of pine woods in Durham, Orange, Chatham, and Alamance counties. The lands were purchased by James B. Duke as a backdrop to a scientific study of forestry.

Careful baseline records kept by the forest's first director, Clarence Korstian, make Duke Forest an inestimable treasure to today's botanists. Duke shares its wealth with scientists from the University of North Carolina at Chapel Hill and NC State University. It also is tolerant of the public's possessive attitude towards the forest. Amateur nature buffs who roam the forest trails are often as fiercely protective of the forest's fragile ecology as the academicians.

The state-owned Hill Demonstration Forest in northern Durham County also welcomes the public onto its 2,460 acres of research timberland. The forest, a favorite haunt of equestrian enthusiasts, was created in 1929 with a gift of 500 acres of land from Durham philanthropist George Watts Hill. He specified that it be used by the (then) new School of Forestry at NC State University. Land acquisition has expanded the forest to include lowlands, wetlands, and part of the Eno River. Hikers, joggers, and picnickers are invited to park their cars outside the forest and enjoy the miles of trails in the forest, including a 250-acre nature preserve that remains untouched by development or research.

In an enclave near Duke Forest lives a collection of strange-looking mammals, vaguely resembling a cross between an opossum and a raccoon. The diminutive animals are prosimians, a rare family of primates that includes lemurs, pottos, and lorises. Researchers at the Duke Primate Center are dedicated to the preservation of these agile little creatures; the public is invited to view them in their Duke habitat. Since the animals are an endangered species, tours are arranged on weekdays and Saturday mornings by appointment only, and there is a modest admission fee.

Chances are good you won't see a lemur roaming the forests of the Eno River lands, but sighting real raccoons and opossums is a definite possibility. The Eno River winds through northern Durham County, with several park sites dotted along the green space. West Point on the Eno, the most highly developed of the parks, features a working gristmill, blacksmith shop, and photography museum. It is also the launch point for "wafting" trips during the summer months and the gathering place for day and nighttime excursions into the depths

of the woods. West Point also hosts Durham's famed Festival for the Eno, held every Fourth of July holiday, which raises money to buy additional parklands along the Eno.

A GLANCE BACKWARDS

In an off-the-beaten-path corner of northern Durham County lies Stagville Center, a preservation site for one of Durham's earliest homes, the Horton Cottage. Estimated to have been built in the 1770s, the cottage was moved from its original location to the present site to serve as an overseer's home for the slave population in the mid-1800s. Paul Cameron, who owned Horton Plantation at the time, ordered a series of slave cabins built behind the cottage, six of which still stand. They represent the state's longest surviving unit of slave quarters, thanks in part to their brick insulation and the efforts of preservationists. As a special treat during the Christmas holidays, Horton Cottage is decorated with period adornments and opened for candlelight tours.

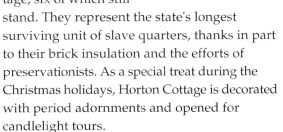

In the enclave near Duke Forest lives a collection of strange looking mammals—prosimians, a rare family of primates that includes lemurs, pottos, and lorises. Courtesy of Durham Convention Center & Visitors Bureau.

Every April, Confederate and Union troops descend on Durham's Bennett Place to reenact the largest surrender of Confederate troops at the end of the War Between the States. The Bennett Place Historical Site is open to visitors throughout the year with a visitors' center, monument, and museum.

Just a few miles away is the restored Duke Homestead, where Washington Duke launched his tobacco empire. The whitewashed Duke farmhouse, with its broad front porch, is set near a renovated tobacco barn. At planting and harvest time, Durham residents don 1800's clothing to work the homestead, make lye soap, bake oven-fired cornbread, and tend the tobacco crop in fields that surround the homestead.

Duke Chapel, the majestic Gothic Revival cathedral named for its benefactor, James B. Duke, is Durham's most famous landmark. Completed in 1932, it took workers nearly two and a half years to build the $2.2 million

chapel. Its 210-foot spire and 50-bell, four-octave carillon can be seen and heard throughout West Campus. Inside the soaring 1,500-seat sanctuary, four organs (including two Flentrops) echo against the Indiana limestone arches. Seventy-seven stained glass windows line the walls—the top windows illustrating the Old Testament; the lower windows the New Testament. During restricted hours, visitors can ride the elevator to the top of the chapel tower for an overview of the campus and downtown Durham.

Durham's entire downtown area has been declared a historic site by the National Register of Historic Places—the first commercial district so designated in North Carolina. Even neophyte students of architecture are dazzled by the ornate brickwork and turn-of-the-century storefronts. The area encompasses Brightleaf Square, a set of restored tobacco warehouses that now houses a thriving shopping area. Shoppers can find everything from CDs to Mexican food at Brightleaf Square, a truly contemporary offering. For shopping on the antique side, try Patterson's Mill Country Store in the southern part of the county. An anachronism by design, Patterson's not only displays and sells some of America's country-store favorites, it features a reconstructed old-time doctor's office and pharmacy.

There are other remnants of Durham's heritage tucked here and there throughout the county: the 103-year-old sanctuary of St. Joseph's AME Church in the Hayti area; Duke's East Campus, which started life as North Carolina's finest racetrack for thoroughbred horses; the Woolworth's lunch counter that witnessed Durham's civil rights sit-ins, now housed at the North Carolina School of Science and Mathematics; and the Georgian buildings that comprise North Carolina Central University. Scratch the surface of almost any neighborhood in Durham and you'll uncover its vibrant past.

All that digging may work up an appetite. Fortunately, Durham is the right place to be hungry! The city boasts several nationally acclaimed restaurants—Magnolia Grill and Nana's among them. Vegetarians love AnotherThyme, and seafood afficionados prefer Fishmongers Fish Market downtown. Some newcomers on the scene that show great promise are Mark's American Cuisine, Parizade, and Foster's Market. But the best loved of all are the hometown restaurants, like Hartman's Steak House, now a Durham institution, and the dozens of places that serve up generous helpings of North Carolina barbeque. This vinegary variation, made with smoked pork and clear, peppery sauce, is served with creamy slaw, an order of Brunswick stew, and piping hot hushpuppies for the most authentic Durham meal in town!

Of course, even the most devoted Durham supporter might develop a bit of wanderlust for some out-of-town fare. Why not a heaping platter of Calabash-style shrimp, fresh from the shrimping boats on North Carolina's Crystal Coast? The addictive lure of the ocean has a simple cure for Durham folks—a short three-hour drive and the clean, sandy panorama stretches for miles, dotted only by seagulls and picturesque lighthouses.

Turn your vehicle in the opposite direction to drink in the majesty of the Great Smoky Mountain range, located just four hours west of Durham. Hiking trails, outdoor Indian performances, and a national park are just a few of the treasures to be discovered in this outdoor paradise. And nearby Asheville hosts America's largest mansion, the Biltmore House, while Charlotte, just to the south, is the home of the new professional football team, the Carolina Panthers. Durham is perfectly sited for adventures to Virginia, South Carolina—and the world, via its international flights from the Raleigh-Durham International Airport.

Clearly, Durham has come a long way since its racetrack and amusement park days. Any remaining nostalgia for yesterday's trolley rides is soothed by the wonderful array of Durham's special treasures. █

█ The Museum of Life and Science is Durham's most visited exhibition. Children can create their own miniature 13-foot tornado. Photo by Bob Hopkins/Impact Photography.

█ Previous page. Duke Chapel, the majestic Gothic Revival Cathedral named for James B. Duke, is Durham's most famous landmark. Photo by Paul Liggitt Photography.

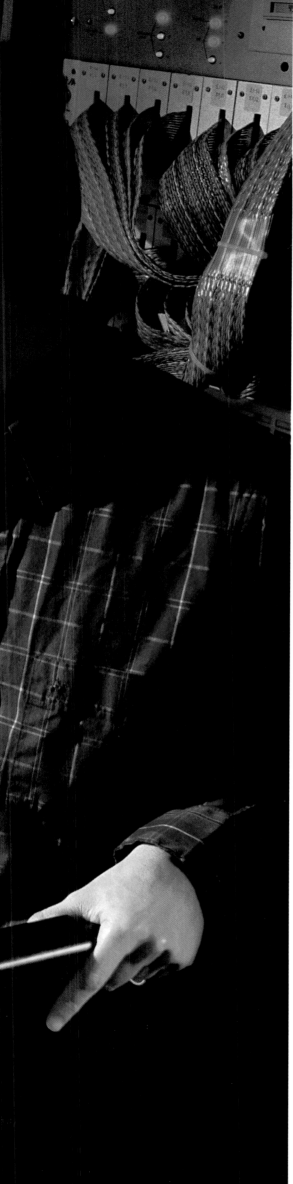

chapter ten

THE FUTURE

From generation to generation, Durham's legacy is passed forward, propelled into the future as surely as the steady tick of its internal clock. That legacy was created by the honest labor of a few dozen men and women, grew to include the Southern graciousness of a midsized city, and is now enriched by the thousands of new arrivals who imprint it with their own lives. It encompasses that most ethereal of desires: high quality of life.

▌"High-tech" has been part of Durham's daily lexicon for years and will continue on the forefront of the ever-advancing frontier of science and technology. Courtesy of Duke University.

"Quality of life" quite nearly defies definition. There are as many meanings imparted to it as people who voice the phrase. Yet there are some abiding commonalities that connect the definitions: quiet streets, safe neighborhoods, friendly people, clean air, efficient transportation, good schools, plentiful housing. Durham answers "yes" to the entire checklist. The question is: can it continue to do so tomorrow?

By the year 2020, Durham's population is projected to top 285,000, a 57 percent increase, with an accompanying 63 percent increase in new jobs. Adding 100,000 people and hundreds of companies to a county the size of Durham could spell disaster for the quality of life, were it not for the forward thinking of Durham's government leaders. In a remarkable coalition, Durham city and county governments, along with citizens from their many neighborhoods, have pulled together a proposal that outlines Durham's options in a blueprint appropriately called the "2020 Plan."
The 2020 Plan tackles the very heart of issues central to healthy growth: water protection, traffic corridors, development, green space. They are issues that won't wait long. "We would be O.K. if we maintained the status quo for five or maybe even 10 years," said Paul Norby, director of the City/County Planning Department. "But we need to make some changes today so that we'll still have a bright future in 15 to 20 years."

High on the priority list is a dramatic increase in roadways. "The travel demand is increasing. We have two to three times as many people driving, and we find that there are more cars per household. Our streets are destined to be more congested," said Keith Luck, city/county principal planner and an architect of the 2020 Plan. Norby agrees. "We just can't build roads fast enough!" he said. The 2020 Plan suggests that 20 percent of residential development in Durham County over the next 30 years be in "compact communities," with mixed-use buildings. Retailers, childcare centers, grocery stores, and small office buildings could be constructed within walking distance of residences, thus reducing the number of car trips needed.

Durham's downtown area is also ripe for development of residential construction. Bill Kalkhof, president of Downtown Durham Inc., works feverishly to reenergize Durham's central city. He is touting downtown as an arts and entertainment complex, with the new baseball stadium and a thriving arts center. But he has also joined forces with Curt Eshelman, M.D. and Allen Wilcox to brainstorm ideas about a downtown vastly different from today's. Still in the preliminary stages, the planning attracted 40 Durham leaders plus interested citizens who spent a week discussing options with an expert in downtown renovation. Possible scenarios include creating a small lake in a downtown valley, building residential single and multifamily homes, and adding shopping and day-to-day services within walking distance of the residences.

Residents could walk to a proposed mass transit hub downtown, board a bus or light

Independence Park, a 250-acre mixed-use development in northern Durham County, is a prime example of the vision of Durham's business leaders. Photo by Bob Hopkins/Impact Photography.

railcar, and arrive at work in Research Triangle Park within minutes. The Triangle Transit Authority, composed of representatives from Durham, Chapel Hill, and Raleigh, is well along in its planning for a regional fixed-transit system that would connect major employers. First on the drawing board for Durham is a route that links Research Triangle Park, South Square Mall, Chapel Hill, Treyburn Corporate Park, and downtown Durham. A similar system in Raleigh could connect with Durham at the Raleigh-Durham International Airport.

Regional cooperation is clearly a part of "tomorrows" in the Triangle. Durham actively participates in regional planning and supports the Research Triangle Regional Partnership, which targets increased economic development. The area has even established a Leadership Triangle program, a spin-off of the leadership programs offered through the individual chambers of commerce. The program helps groom regional leaders for cooperative civic opportunities.

The net effect of all this planning is to retain much of Durham's best-loved attributes. "I still want my 10-minute commute to work!" said Kalkhof. "That's one of the things that makes this a great place to live."

Becky Heron, chair of the Durham County Commissioners and a 35-year resident, says those quality of life issues will continue to attract new people to Durham. "I see a bright, progressive future for Durham. Just look at what we have to offer," she said. "We have more activities in the community than people can participate in; we have open green space, plenty of good, clean water. And we have made efforts to protect those things that make us so attractive."

Whether they are drawn by the easygoing, southern lifestyle or the compelling employment climate, more and more newcomers are discovering Durham's special charm. As they build homes, raise families, and join the community, they, like the city founders, will help guide Durham's destiny with their own brand of intensity and passion.

Previous page. At the threshold of the doorway to discovery. Durham's children help propel the community toward an even brighter future. Photo by Bob Hopkins/Impact Photography.

Durham offers countless opportunities for tranquil moments. Photo by Paul Liggitt Photography.

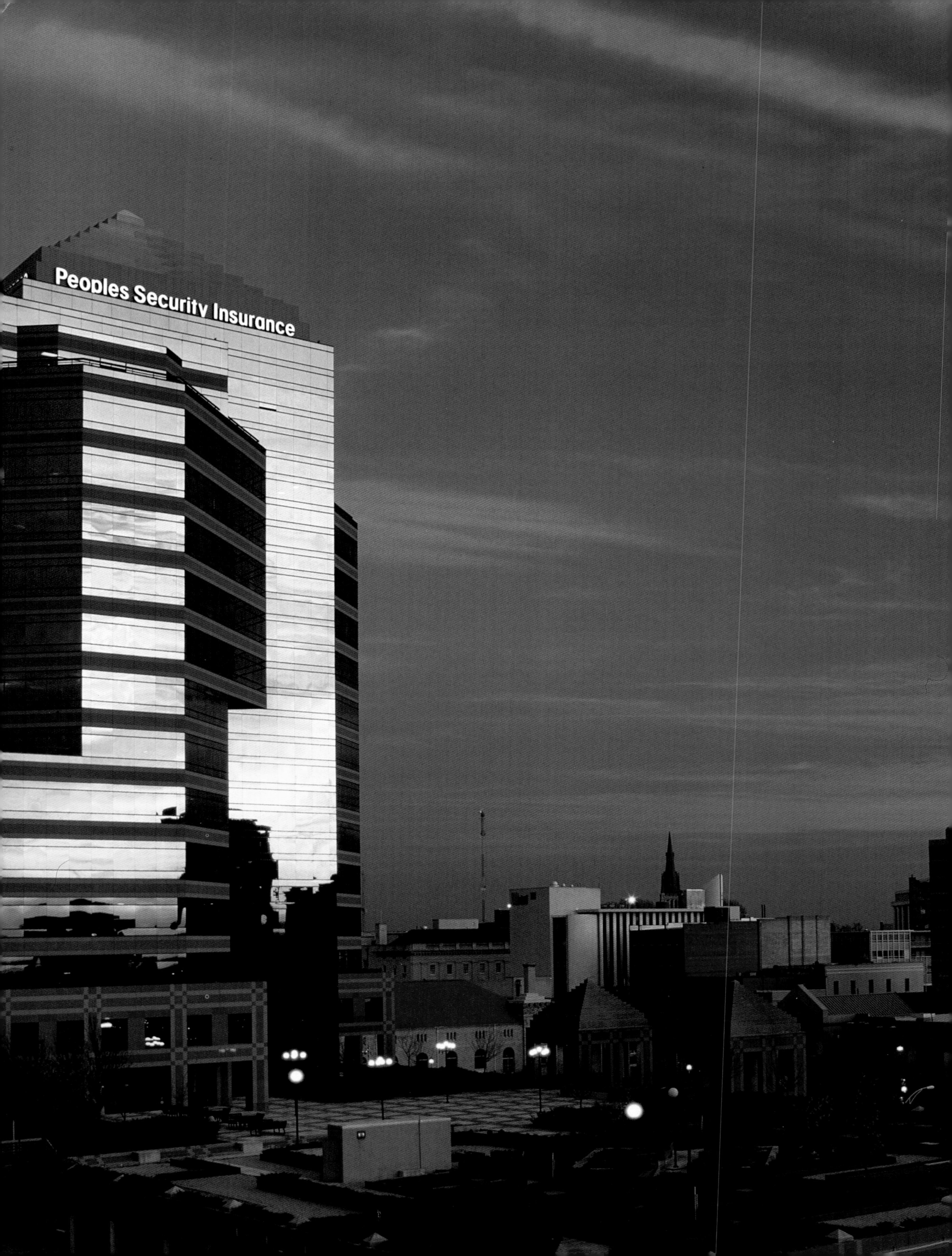
Peoples Security Insurance

PART TWO
durham's enterprises

chapter eleven
NETWORKS

▌ The area's communication and energy firms are responsible for the networking which keeps people, information, and power circulating inside and outside the Durham area. Photo by Paul Liggitt Photography.

With roots that stretch back more than 100 years and a staunch commitment to providing Durham with the best source of news and

advertising, The Durham Herald Company is enthusiastic about its second century of service to its community. The phenomenal success of this vigorous company stems, in part, from continuity of local ownership that has encouraged exceedingly high journalistic standards.

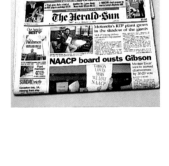

"The Durham Herald Company has thrived as a result of our mission to provide Durham with a first-rate local newspaper," said Richard J. Kaspar, president and publisher. "In this world of conglomerates, we remain under essentially the same Durham ownership that has served the community for more than 100 years."

It was the founding of the Durham *Morning Herald* in 1894 that eventually led to creation of the company. In 1895, Joe H. King and Edward Tyler Rollins formed a partnership called The Durham Herald Company which published the *Morning Herald*. Twenty-three years later, the company became a closed-stock corporation, with King and Rollins as the sole stockholders. That same year, 1918, King sold half his stock to Rollins and the other half to Carl C. Council. The Durham Herald Company is still an independent, locally owned newspaper nearly 80 years later.

Today's *The Herald-Sun* is the result of a 1991 merger between the *Durham Morning Herald* and *The Durham Sun*. *The Durham Sun* was founded in 1889; the *Durham Morning Herald* acquired it in 1929, maintaining it as a separate afternoon newspaper. Every day, The Durham Herald Company publishes *The Herald-Sun* and a zoned daily edition, *The Chapel Hill Herald*. Each week, the daily editions reach 74 percent of all Durham adults; while, the Sunday editions reach 79 percent each month.

The Herald-Sun offers a broad spectrum of information that includes local, national, and international news. Special sections—Sports, Durham, Life, Food, Business, Wheels, Insight, Real Estate, and University—are targeted to specific audiences in the Durham area. The company maintains bureaus in Chapel Hill, Hillsborough, Roxboro, and Raleigh to stay on top of news throughout the Triangle.

In addition to daily newspapers, the company publishes *Preview*, a weekly entertainment section which is distributed on Fridays. Our weekly newspapers like *The Durham Express* and *The Raleigh Extra* reach 36,000 households in Durham and 41,000 Wake County homes, respectively.

The owners, publisher, and editors of *The Herald-Sun* live and work in Durham, allowing them a keen understanding of the community. Collectively, they keep a finger on the pulse of the newspaper's readership, a factor in making *The Herald-Sun* Durham's dominant newspaper.

"We are Durham's newspaper because Durham is our community," said William E. N. Hawkins, vice president and executive editor. "We have added staff and news sections to *The Herald-Sun* to serve the changing interests of readers. Our hard work has paid off with numerous state and national awards. And our innovative color television page was selected as the best daily television page in America in 1994."

Vibrant color arrived in 1990 via a new $9 million Goss Headliner offset press. The press permits vastly improved color control and photographic reproduction which allows us to produce the most colorful newspapers in North Carolina. The lightning-fast Goss Headliner can print as many as 72,000, 48-page newspapers per hour! And to conserve newsprint, a computerized press control system reads page negatives before printing so that adjustments in variables (such as ink values) can be made before paper is wasted. Not only does the effort save money for the company by keeping newspaper prices lower, the conservation effort is good for the environment, another top priority for the company. The Durham Herald Company is one of the top newspapers in the country in the use of recycled newsprint for its daily and Sunday newspapers.

The company takes its commitment to Durham seriously—through dollars and people. When the company moved from its long-time downtown location to a new 13.2-acre site on Pickett Road, it spent in excess of $27 million on the project, helping to fuel the local economy. "The Durham Herald Company has invested heavily in Durham," Kaspar said. "But we have also invested in quality employees who are committed to the mission of being the essential and trusted source of news and advertising for the entire community. Thanks to that commitment, we are a growing newspaper in what is surely one of the most vibrant communities in the state and nation."

The Durham Herald Company values the contributions of its 375 employees, who reciprocate its trust with loyalty. The average tenure at the company is seven years, and a number of employees are second- or third-generation members of the original Herald Sun family. Also vital to the company's success are part-time employees, correspondents, independent newspaper carriers, and contract haulers. Working together in a deadline business creates deep and lasting friendships. Even the newspaper's retirees maintain close ties with the company.

Dozens of employees of the firm also reach out to the community, offering their time and money to schools, churches, civic clubs, and public service campaigns. Some of the events and programs that benefit from their involvement are: Habitat For Humanity, Front Page Awards, the Festival for the Eno, the Fourth of July Fireworks, the PAC-6 Basketball Tournament, Centerfest, the Bull Durham Blues Festival, and Share Your Christmas.

The Durham Herald Company reaches out in print, too, with the publication of more than 20 "niche" publications, mostly for not-for-profit agencies such as WUNC (*Listen* magazine), the North Carolina Museum of Life

and Science (*Adventures*), and the Greater Durham Chamber of Commerce (*ACTION*).

Those publications and others that cover health, business, and the arts reflect the changing face of Durham. A century ago, when King and Rollins formed their partnership, Durham was strictly a textile and tobacco town. Today, the area is a national leader in education, health, and technology. *The Herald-Sun* has kept pace with its community, and those involved with the newspaper understand that its future and Durham's are inexorably linked.

"These are exciting times for Durham and *The Herald-Sun*," Kaspar said. "We know that the next century will bring major changes in the way information is delivered. What will not change is our commitment to remain as the dominant source of news and advertising for our community."

In today's competitive economic marketplace, corporate decision-makers seek locations, both facilities and communities, that have a dynamic and sophisticated infrastructure to support their respective operations. In a locale such as the Research Triangle, it is imperative that service providers furnish state-of-the-art services and delivery capacity. In that regard, GTE is a truly outstanding service provider of telecommunications, in every sense of the word.

-Tom White
Vice-President, Economic Development
Durham Chamber of Commerce

In 1955, GTE merged with the owner of the Durham Telephone Company and began providing local telephone service to the Durham/ Research Triangle Park area. Over the next four decades, GTE became an integral factor in Durham's exciting economic evolution. With an eye towards the area's tremendous economic potential, GTE has deployed in Durham one of the most advanced telecommunications networks available.

GTE's widespread use of fiber optic cable, 100 percent digital switching, including ATM (Asynchronous Transfer Mode), and the rapid spread of SONET (Synchronous Optical Network) electronics have brought the telecommunications future to Durham today—far in advance of most areas of the state and nation.

America's first statewide information highway is being built in North Carolina; the inaugural users came on-line in 1994. GTE joined Southern Bell, Sprint/Mid-Atlantic Telecom, other local exchange companies, and AT&T in a unique team effort to service the first information highway customer: the State of North Carolina. The state is using the highway's broadband capacities

■ GTE's Network Operations Center in Texas makes sure millions of calls get through perfectly, day and night, in Durham and across the United States.

for distance teaching in schools and colleges, for medical applications like teleradiology and distance diagnosis, and for improving government efficiency, crime control, and broadbased economic development. GTE brought on-line the highway's very first end-user—MCNC (Microelectronics Center of North Carolina)— in Research Triangle Park (RTP). Two of the state's first 10 ATM switches were placed in Durham County. GTE's ATM Market Trial was the state's first regulatory permission to bring business customers onto the Highway's infrastructure.

An exemplary user of its own technology, GTE has enhanced services to customers while streamlining its operations to keep costs low. This internal "process re-engineering" effort set the industry standard, positioning GTE as a market leader in the voice, video, and data arenas.

Throughout this companywide effort, GTE maintained its investment focus on Durham, adding a regional bill distribution center, a national interexchange carrier center, and the multistate South Branch Sales headquarters. Durham also became one of GTE's 10 regional headquarters, as well as headquarters for the Southeast Division. GTE MobilNet, GTE Supply, GTE Leasing, GTE Directories, and GTE Government Systems operate offices in Durham.

■*DURHAM IS SITE FOR ADVANCED TRIALS*

Durham's sophisticated residential and business customer base provides a fertile testing ground for many GTE products and services. Two RTP companies successfully completed one of the nation's first Personal Communications System trials—GTE TeleGo®—a combination wireline and wireless service.

The VistaNet project, an alliance among GTE, Southern Bell, the University of North Carolina Medical Center, and MCNC, demonstrated how the power of the Cray computer could be utilized for a cancer patient undergoing radiation therapy by offering pinpoint accuracy about dosage and location.

A Durham subdivision, Sunningdale, became one of the nation's first recipients of fiber optic "fiber-to-the-curb," facilitating residential connection to advanced, high-speed services.

Durham, including RTP, was the first test

site for GTE's "World Class Network" bundle of advanced business telecommunication services. High-speed data transport services, such as SMDS, MMDS, and fast packet switching; ISDN (Integrated Services Digital Network), a key enabler of telecommuting; Video Connect; and MetroLAN (a competitive pricing structure) are among offerings. With GTE, RTP grew from the world's largest telecommunications SmartPark into the first site of the next generation World Class Network.

In 1988, GTE introduced in Durham the state's first regional calling plan—TriWide^{SM}. The immensely popular service significantly reduced the cost of calling within the Triangle area using seven-digit dialing.

As part of its company-wide commitment to value-added customer service, GTE used the industry's rapidly advancing technology to create solutions to customers' needs. GTE's Service Performance Guarantee was the first to be introduced nationally, demonstrating the company's desire to benchmark the quality of its service as well as its products.

GTE REMAINS A LEADING CORPORATE CITIZEN

Clearly, GTE's telecommunications contributions have been an important factor in Durham's economic success and enviable quality of life. GTE has also been a leading corporate citizen through its community involvement and philanthropic efforts. The company has offered substantial support to nonprofit organizations, especially in the areas of education and economic development, and has been a leader in both corporate and employee giving to the United Way.

GTE employees sit on boards of many community organizations and devote thousands of hours to social welfare, the arts, and education. The GTE Foundation, regional grants, and local grants funnel approximately $300,000 annually into worthy Durham efforts.

CORPORATE ROOTS ARE TRACED TO 1918

GTE's corporate roots can be traced to Wisconsin's Richland Center Telephone Company, which was founded in 1918. Associated Telephone Company of California was soon brought into the fold, and the company was renamed the Associated Telephone Utilities Company.

Expansion was halted by the stock market crash of 1929, but after a period of decline, the company was reorganized in 1935 as General Telephone Corporation. The new company experienced unprecedented growth over the next few decades. A 1955 merger with the Midwest's Theodore Gary and Company virtually doubled the company's operating revenues and brought the company its first international telephone operations. In the biggest telecommunications merger in history, GTE joined with Contel in 1991.

In the 1990s, the GTE Corporation encompasses: Telephone Operations; Personal Communications Services including GTE MobilNet, Contel Cellular, and GTE Airfone; GTE Government Systems; GTE Laboratories; and GTE Information Services, including GTE Directories.

GTE Corporation is the largest U.S.-based local telephone company and the second-largest mobile cellular carrier—providing voice, video, and data products and services over 22 million access lines in portions of the United States, Canada, the Caribbean, South America, and the Pacific. On a global scale, GTE is the fourth-largest publicly owned telecommunications company in the world.

Through ISDN (Integrated Services Digital Network), GTE can bring interactive video and other advanced capabilities to home computer screens in Durham. ISDN is one of the advanced business services demonstrated at GTE's Technology Solutions Center in Research Triangle Park.

GTE began deploying fiber optic cable in the early 1980s in Durham and Research Triangle Park. Fiber optic cable is the backbone of GTE's advanced voice, video and data services.

Durham and Cellular One were tailor-made for each other. "Durham's electronically sophisticated population welcomes the mobile

CELLULAR ONE

convenience of cellular service," says Karen Puckett, vice president and general manager of GTE Mobilnet's Southeast Region, which operates under the Cellular One name.

"Durham attracts high-tech workers, so the people who live and work here are naturals for our services," Puckett said. "And in addition to business use, families have come to value cellular as a way of checking on the safety and security of family members."

Cellular One, originally owned by the Providence Journal Publishing Company, began offering cellular service to the Triangle in 1985. In 1990, the firm was purchased by GTE Mobilnet, a wholly owned subsidiary of GTE Corporation (the largest U.S.-based telephone company and the nation's second-largest cellular service provider). Today, the cellular industry has more than 23 million subscribers nationwide; 38,000 new subscribers sign up every business day.

Locally, Cellular One subscribers are served by the regional office, which provides engineering, marketing, distribution, customer care, financial services, and human resources support for the Durham area plus 12 additional southeastern markets. The more than 250 employees who work in the Cellular One regional office and two area sales offices have a common goal: to furnish a selection of services that fits every type of consumer. "We pride ourselves on providing the solutions to consumers' needs, both business and personal," said Puckett. "Cellular gives them real-time accessibility to clients and families."

Accessibility is the name of the game at Cellular One. Nationwide automatic call delivery is available in more than 3,300 cities through the Cellular One network. The abundance of local technologically advanced companies made Durham and the Triangle an ideal location for the introduction of Cellular One's

Cellular One provides the latest technology in wireless data transmission.

innovative voice, video, and data services. "New Options in Wireless" (NOW) includes "Find Me Now"—a system that allows callers to reach a Cellular One customer by calling a single number. The system can be programmed to search for the customer in four locations.

"Video Now" allows users to transmit captured video over the Cellular One network from remote locations. WRAL-TV in nearby Raleigh uses this new technology for news broadcasting. With "Databridge Now," users can access data from computer networks without modification of the host site. These state-of-the-art services can help users increase productivity and reduce business costs, reports Puckett.

Cellular One stays involved in the local community, as well as the electronic airwaves. Puckett reports that Cellular One employees volunteer in such Durham programs as Habitat for Humanity and Toys for Tots. Cellular One also co-sponsors the Duke Children's Classic, United Way, and Special Olympics. That commitment to Durham will continue to grow with the community and Cellular One.

Since Durham is ranked as one of the best places in the country to live and work, Cellular One expects sustained expansion. "Cellular is growing across the country, and it will continue to grow," said Puckett. "Durham is a growing market, driven by the type of people who live and work here and their willingness to embrace cellular as a personal communication tool."

Cellular One's network technicians are constantly planning for cellular expansion and system enhancement.

Distribution line technicians installing equipment to serve the fast growing Triangle Area.

When James B. Duke, Dr. Gill Wylie, and William S. Lee formed the Southern Power Company in the Catawba River area in 1905, they had no idea there would be a vast market for services to commercial and residential customers. The company expanded west and east expecting to sell power to industry, but found those industries wanted the company to provide electric power to residential communities and small businesses as well. Southern Power obliged, expanding its customer base several-fold.

The Southern Power Company became Duke Power Company in 1924 and today serves the Piedmont sections of North Carolina and South Carolina. The company's service area begins in Anderson, South Carolina, and follows the I-85 corridor as far north and east as Durham. Along the way, it provides electricity to major cities that include Greenville, Spartanburg, Charlotte, Winston-Salem, Greensboro, and Burlington.

Durham citizens are served by the Triangle-area Duke Power operation, which supplies electric service to Durham County, Orange County, and south Granville County, with a work force of about 250. Although Duke Power Company's corporate headquarters is in Charlotte, the company maintains local headquarters at the corner of Chapel Hill and Duke streets in downtown Durham. A Duke Power operations center is located on Highway 70 West.

Duke Power Company's roots were firmly planted in Durham through the company's affiliation with the Duke family, but it was the 1950s before the company moved to town. Until then, Durham was electrified by Durham Public Service, which provided both electric

and gas utilities to the city. Duke Power Company purchased Durham Public Service, promptly selling off the natural gas division. The purchase also included acquisition of Durham's city-wide transit service—electric trolley cars in the early days and later gas—and diesel-fired buses. Duke Power Company sold the transit system to the City of Durham in 1990.

Today, the numbers tell an impressive story about a company that has made a habit of listening to its customers and responding to their needs. Duke Power Company now supplies electricity to 1.7 million customers in a 20,000-square-mile service area, making it the seventh-largest investor-owned utility in the United States. It operates 3 nuclear generating stations, 8 coal-fired stations, and 27 hydroelectric stations. Together, these units produce 84 billion kilowatt hours of electricity, with total electric revenues in 1994 of $4.3 billion.

Growth brings new challenges to Duke Power Company, and one such challenge is to serve the exacting specifications of high-technology industries in the Research Triangle Park. Although a millisecond voltage fluctuation has virtually no effect on an electric motor, for instance, it makes a significant impact on an updated, digitized system. Duke Power is committed to continuous improvements that increase reliability for these demanding electrical tasks.

Deregulation of the electric utility industry has posed an even greater challenge. Duke Power Company both recognizes and addresses issues of reducing costs, improving service, and expanding business opportunities in its nonregulated businesses. The company's reputation as a well-run electric utility was built on its ability to design, construct, operate, and maintain low-cost generating facilities. Today, the company seeks to sell that expertise across the country and throughout the world. 🖎

Duke officials discussing power quality solutions required in the highly technical Research Triangle area.

Experience matters. Whether you're talking about a family doctor or a television news team, it

WTVD-TV CHANNEL 11

takes years of experience to do a job well. Here in the place we call the Heart of Carolina, you'll find that kind of experience in the team from WTVD, NewsChannel 11. A treasured resource in the community for over 40 years, WTVD provides news, entertainment, and public service to viewers in a 23-county area of central North Carolina.

WTVD flickered to life on area television screens in the fall of 1954. Founded by a group of area businessmen, the station soon became part of a new company now known as Capital Cities/ABC, Inc. Today, that makes WTVD part of one of the world's largest media companies, an organization that includes the ABC television network, ESPN, several metropolitan newspapers, and a chain of television and radio stations across the country.

Still, WTVD's focus remains uniquely local. In fact, the Capital Cities/ABC business philosophy centers around the idea of decentralization. So decisions that affect the station are always made locally, by the men and women who live and work here. And over the years, they've built a community asset that viewers have learned to rely on.

The station now operates out of four locations in the region, maintaining offices in Durham, Raleigh, Fayetteville, and Wilson. State-of-the-art technology allows WTVD to broadcast live from anywhere in the region, or indeed anywhere in the world.

But investment in hardware is only half the story. The people of NewsChannel 11 are the real key to its service in the community. Over 140 people, from engineers and technicians to writers and account executives, make up the WTVD family. Of those, the journalists in the

NewsChopper 11, one of the many high-tech tools used to bring news and information to Heart of Carolina viewers.

news department are, of course, the most visible, and their work in many ways defines WTVD's mission—to help viewers understand and make sense of the issues that impact their lives.

Larry Stogner and Miriam Thomas lead the news team, each bringing decades of experience to the anchor desk. In addition to anchoring the 5 p.m., 6 p.m., and 11 p.m. newscasts, both lead active lives in the community. George Mallet and Monica Shuman anchor the 5:30 broadcast and Jennifer Julian is the NewsChannel 11 Troubleshooter. A very popular feature with viewers, Jennifer rolls up her sleeves and actively helps viewers resolve consumer problems. WTVD also maintains a full-time medical reporter, Healthcast 11's Jennifer Silverman. Meteorologist Bill Reh heads the Accu-Weather Center, a facility packed with the latest computer gear, including Doppler 11 radar. And its reporting staff is by far the most experienced group of journalists working for any local station.

Experience. When you add everything up, that's the element that makes WTVD, NewsChannel 11, unique. As viewing choices expand, it seems people in the Heart of Carolina agree...experience does matter. That's why they choose the team with experience from WTVD, NewsChannel 11.

Larry Stogner and Miriam Thomas lead the area's most experienced news team and anchor WTVD's 5, 6, and 11pm newscasts.

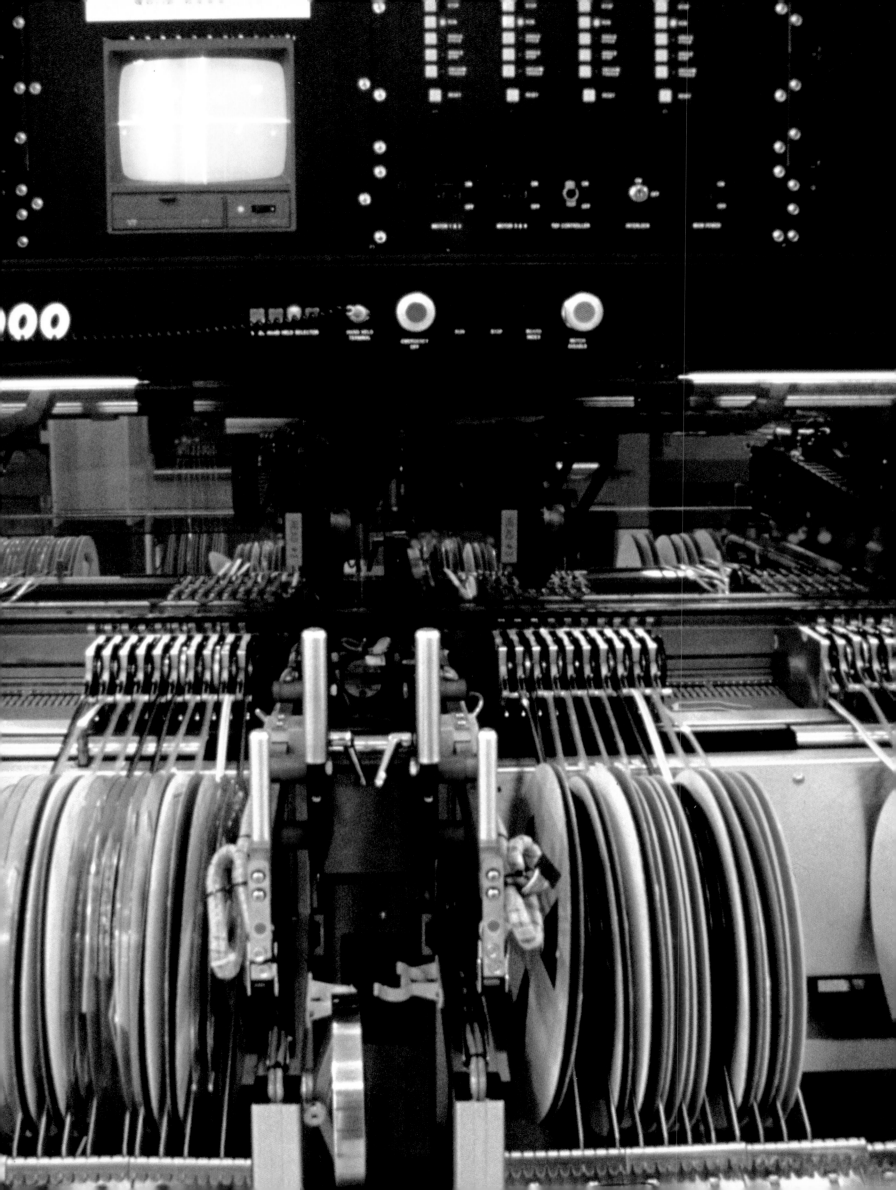

chapter twelve
INDUSTRY
12

Producing goods and services for individuals, Durham manufacturing firms provide employment for many area residents.
Photo courtesy of Nortel.

If you live in North Carolina, chances are your telephone service is supplied by a Nortel Digital Multiplex Switching (DMS) system.

N O R T E L

The systems are actually sophisticated computers used by telephone companies to route the millions of calls placed every day. The DMS system used in your local telephone office, along with about half of all such systems sold nationwide, was manufactured close to home, in Nortel's Research Triangle Park (RTP) facility.

Nortel is a global manufacturer of fully digital telecommunications switching equipment. The company pioneered the development of the switching systems in the 1970s; the popularity of the new technology dramatically boosted the capacity of Nortel's manufacturing and research and development facilities in North Carolina. The company's rapid expansion in North Carolina parallels its exponential growth across the U.S. telecommunications market. Based in Ontario, Canada, Nortel opened its U.S. headquarters in Boston in 1971.

Checking signals on circuit packs in the Hardware Design Lab.

The company's first digital switch, the DMS-10, was manufactured in Creedmoor, North Carolina, and installed in Fort White, Florida, in 1977. The switch is still in service, with appropriate upgrades that incorporate the latest technology. The development of a larger switch, the DMS-100, led Nortel to open a 250,000-square-foot office and manufacturing facility on 60 acres in RTP in 1980. The building has been expanded twice and now has 660,000 square feet of space.

In addition, the company's research and development subsidiary, Bell Northern Research (BNR), and the Data Networks Division occupy even more RTP facilities. Supplemental office and manufacturing space is located in the Imperial Center just outside RTP. And in Raleigh, the company's Technical Education Center offers instruction to customers, as well as telephone company and Nortel employees.

Nortel marked its 100th anniversary in 1995 and celebrated this milestone with the official adoption of a new name. Northern Telecom became Nortel on April 27 of that year. This shorter, crisper logo reflected the company's expanding role as a unified organization and a global resource for customers and consolidated its image throughout the world.

The 100th anniversary also offered an opportunity to look to the future while celebrating the company's rich heritage. From its beginnings as a small Canadian telephone equipment company, Nortel has traveled far during this century. Today, the company's goal is to be the leading architect of global communications networks. To accomplish that goal, Nortel has set its sights on other world markets. From its secure North American base, the company is expanding rapidly in the Caribbean and into Europe. As these markets mature and stabilize, future areas of growth also are emerging: Japan, China, and Eastern Europe.

In addition to Nortel's globalization efforts, the company has initiated new business directions and organizational structures. Such change is nothing new to Nortel. During its first 100 years, the company demonstrated an indomitable spirit of flexibility, adaptability, innovation, and a willingness to recreate itself as the need arose. Throughout its history, Nortel has been adept at turning change into opportunity, which is why the company founded by a New England sea captain and a handful of good workmen became a world leader.

Back in 1880, former sea captain Charles Sise created The Bell Telephone Company of Canada in Montreal. The following year, he lost his domestic supply of telephone equipment, and because the Canadian patent law demanded that he use a Canadian supplier or lose patent rights, he opened his own manufacturing plant. In 1882, the manufacturing branch of The Bell Telephone Company of Canada was born. It flourished and was incorporated as a separate company in 1895. That company, Northern Electric and Manufacturing Company Limited, is the true, legal ancestor of Nortel.

Nortel makes its home in Research Triangle Park.

Pillar of Support Award to the company for 10 years of outstanding support.

As Nortel enters its second century, the company recognizes that the information industry has become highly advanced and extremely competitive. At Nortel, however, it's business as usual—designing, building, and integrating a world of dynamically evolving information, entertainment, and communications networks. Those networks allow the company to deliver customer solutions that transform daily lives, from basic telephone service in developing countries to employee access across time zones. Nortel conducts business by putting customers first and helping them succeed.

Nortel recognizes that the world of networks alone won't hold its place at the forefront of the global information industry. Dedicated employees who are focused on customers, combined with advanced technology, however, will help the company meet the challenges of tomorrow. Satisfying the ever-expanding and ever-evolving needs of its customers is clearly Nortel's primary route to maintaining its leadership role in the global marketplace of the 21st century. 🖉

Today, Nortel employs about 60,000 people throughout the world and has global revenues in excess of $8 billion. Nortel and BNR, the company's research and development subsidiary, employ more than 8,000 people in North Carolina. In addition to providing a solid employment base, the company has developed strong community relationships.

The Nortel/BNR community relations program addresses a legitimate need by focusing on public education reform. The company's partnership with Johnston County Schools has become a model throughout the state. Major activities include computer training for teachers and staff by Nortel employee volunteers, business partner in the N.C. Total Quality Education pilot, and in-kind contributions of more than $700,000.

Other education-related involvement includes training of administrative staff at Raleigh's Enloe High School and the Hillside High School Mentoring Program. The BNR laboratory has a VideoMeet Program that allows local students to discuss topics with students in England and Canada on everything from the information highway to acid rain.

The Nortel Teacher Training Program won the company the Best in Class Award from The Conference Board of New York in 1994. During the same year, Nortel received three Corporate Support of the Arts awards. In addition, INROADS/NC Triangle, Inc. gave the

Every person's job is extremely important.

The growth and export of tobacco has played a major role in the development of the American economy. Durham's own tobacco company, Liggett & Myers, has had a huge impact on the city and its surrounding area for over a hundred years.

LIGGETT GROUP INC.

"I came to work here in 1991, so I'm a relative newcomer to this area," said Ronald Bernstein, executive vice president and chief financial officer. "It didn't take me long to appreciate the role tobacco and Liggett played in building Durham."

Indeed, Durham was a sleepy little town until after the Civil War when Washington Duke returned home from the battlefields to establish a cigarette factory. That industry would grow to become one of the largest industries in the world. In the years after the war, numerous tobacco factories came into existence. Washington Duke's American Tobacco Company absorbed most, including Liggett in 1899, and Durham took pride in its world-wide reputation for producing fine tobacco products. In 1911, the courts forced American to dissolve its tobacco manufacturing monopoly and Liggett re-emerged as a separate company.

The sweet smell of tobacco being processed at Liggett continues to waft over downtown Durham as it has for the past century. Each

Many cornerstones throughout the Liggett complex predate the turn of the century.

year high-speed machines turn out billions of brand name cigarettes, such as Chesterfield, Lark, L&M, and Eve, and "price value" cigarettes. Liggett, which has always enjoyed a reputation for innovation, introduced the generic concept in the early 1980s. This plain label cigarette revolutionized the industry spawning a whole new category now known as "price value". Liggett continues its market innovation in specialized marketing programs for a variety of price value brands it produces. Pyramid, Covington, Epic, Kingsport, Meridian, and a host of other brands are manufactured and creatively marketed to fill special "niches" in the cigarette marketplace.

Liggett takes pride in the thousands of employees who, throughout its history, have worked at Liggett and played a vital role in shaping this community into what it is today. Liggett's leadership is etched into everthing from the Durham Arts Council, to the Hotel/Civic Center complex, to the Duke Children's Classic of which it is the the founding sponsor. In addition to a substantial payroll, the over $30 million in goods and services purchased from area vendors provides Durham's economy with a vital boost.

"We have a strong history of leadership, contributions, and employee involvement in the community," said Bernstein. "It pleases me greatly that Liggett is carrying on the tobacco tradition in Durham and our legacy of community service." ✐

Liggett employees are proud to be a part of a company with such a wonderful history.

Back in 1965, Paul Reaves had a solid background in paint contracting and distribution—and a budding idea—to start his own paint sundries company. By the end of the year, Reaves and Company, Inc. was a reality. Thirty years later, the company has three downtown Durham locations with 105 employees which produce professional accessories ranging from drop cloths to gloves to disposable coveralls and car covers.

Reaves and Company ships its "Big Ram" painters' products all over the United States and to several foreign markets. Eighteen grades of canvas, plastic, and paper drop cloths are supplied to large accounts and to small, independent paint stores. The firm is the country's largest producer of paint strainers, spray socks, and painters' mitts. "We're a highly specialized, low-profile business," Reaves said. "We're probably better known in California, which is our major market, than we are here in Durham."

Reaves and Company's target market is professional painters; development of a new product often stems from observing painters on the job. A prime example of a painter-inspired new product is an improved bag-type paint strainer/filter. Traditional versions of the strainer required two people—one to pour, one to hold the bag while the paint was poured through. "So we said, why not sew elastic around the top of the filter and secure it to the paint bucket?" Reaves said. "Now, 75 percent of all filters have the elastic top. It was a small, innovative idea that was a big success."

Another success story is a "Polyduk" drop cloth that absorbs paint on one side, but is coated with polyethylene on the other to prevent leakage. And when Reaves noticed that spray painters constantly fought the fine paint mist that settled in their hair and inside their clothes, he had another brainstorm. Now spray painters stay out of the mist with the famous Reaves and Company spray sock, a knit, tube-type covering that's effective and comfortable. The company has patented other innovations, such

REAVES & COMPANY, INC.

as a specialized car cover and a box-type paint filter.

Clearly, Reaves and Company is a leader in the paint sundries field, but the company has set its sights on increasing market share by expanding its product line into the large 2-step distributors. These distributors in turn supply thousands of dealers who service and supply the professional painting contractor. "Historically, we like to go where the professional painter goes," Reaves said. "Our biggest customer has more than 3,000 stores and sells specifically to paint professionals."

Reaves believes it is especially important for a local business that trades nationally to be part of its home community. As a Durham native and a graduate of the University of North Carolina at Chapel Hill (thus the "Big Ram" trademark), he takes his community ties seriously. Civic clubs, country club and church, the Chamber of Commerce, and the universities have all benefited from Reaves and Company's service to the community. "We're very supportive of different facets of the community and are an integral part of it," Reaves said.

Front row(L to R): Paula P. Pickard, Corporate Secretary; Paul H. Reaves, President; Charles D. Reaves, Administrative Vice President; Richard T. Riggsbee, National Sales Manager. Back row(L to R): James F. Ward, Vice President - Manufacturing; Ronald M. Johnson, Plant Manager; Alvis F. Warren, Treasurer.

More than 75 years ago, in the bitter atmosphere of Pikes Peak, General Electric (GE) fired up a 350-horsepower, turbosupercharged engine and entered the business of making airplanes fly higher, faster, and more efficiently than ever before.

That mountaintop test landed GE's first aviation-related government contract and paved the way for GE to become a world leader in jet engine technology.

Today, GE Aircraft Engines (GEAE) designs, develops, and manufactures jet engines for a broad spectrum of military and commercial aircraft, and produces aeroderivative engines for marine and industrial (M&I) applications.

GE's quality extends to overseas customers.

Over the years, GEAE has scored many industry firsts. Among them: America's first jet and turboprop engines, the first engines to fly at two and three times the speed of sound, and the first high bypass turbofan engine.

The company scored another first on February 2, 1995, with certification of the world's most powerful engine, the new GE90. The engine was certified by the FAA at 84,700 pounds thrust, and the engine flew on the new twin-engine Boeing 777 for the first time that same day. The GE90 underwent one of the most extensive certification test programs ever undertaken by an engine manufacturer and, during ground testing, achieved a record-breaking 110,000 pounds of thrust.

GEAE launched the GE90 development program in 1990 and, in 1992, chose its facilities in

Durham, North Carolina, to serve as the final assembly and test site for the engine. Durham's highly qualified technical workforce and the layout of the facilities, which can easily accommodate an engine the size of the GE90, made it an ideal site. In 1993, the company transferred assembly of its highly successful CF6-80C2 product line to Durham as well.

The CF6-80C2 is the undisputed industry leader in terms of reliability and fuel efficiency. The engine has been selected to power more than half of the current-generation Airbus Industrie A300 and A310, Boeing 747 and 767, and McDonnell Douglas MD-11 wide-body aircraft currently in service or on order.

The CF6-80 was the first engine in aviation history to receive 180-minute ETOPS (Extended-range Twin-engine OPerationS) approval, thus allowing airlines to use twin-engine, CF6-80-powered aircraft on routes that traditionally required three-and four-engine aircraft.

The GE90 represents GEAE's investment in the future wide-body aircraft market. The engine combines advanced technology with the best proven technology from GE's commercial, military, and joint NASA development programs to provide a highly reliable, fuel-efficient powerplant for the next generation of wide-body aircraft. The GE90-powered Boeing 777 entered service with British Airways in 1995. Total GE90 orders to date are valued at more than $1.5 billion.

GEAE is one of 12 businesses of the General Electric Company and generated nearly $6 billion in sales in 1994. Exports accounted for more than $2 billion of this total. Commercial aircraft engine sales, only a small percentage of the business in the 1970s, today make up 52 percent of GEAE's revenues, while the military engine and M&I operations account for 36 percent and 12 percent, respectively. There are nearly 50,000 GE commercial, military, and M&I engines currently in service with more than 500 customers worldwide.

Pride and commitment go into each GE Aircraft Engine .

When Mitsubishi Semiconductor America, Inc. (MSAI) opened its first facility in Durham in 1983, it was a small plant that tested memory chips from Japan. A modest 16 employees were on the Mistubishi Semiconductor payroll. Subsequent capital investment and expansion have added a design center, wafer fabrication facility and assembly operations to the test function...now enabling the company to control the production of chips from beginning to end. Today, over 500 employees are employed at the Northern Durham location which is Mitsubishi Electric Company's largest capital investment outside Japan. Diligent care and attention to detail by MSAI's employees plus state-of-the-art equipment, high quality materials, and efficient production methods produce reliable semiconductors of superior quality.

MSAI produces a combination of chips and memory modules with a production capaciity of 3.5 million devices per month. The Mistubishi Electric family of manufacturing sites, including MSAI, is recognized as one of the best semiconductor producers in the world with a world-wide ranking in the top ten of all such manufacturers. The individual chips are used in personal computers and workstations, laser printers, telecommunications equipment, office automation equipment, mainframe computers, and industrial equipment.

For specialized applications used in high volume, the company will even design a custom chip, MCU, or application specific memories such as Cache DRAM and 3D RAM. MSAI's design center offers design and research services, which often give the firm an edge in the highly competitive marketplace. The center also conducts research projects which include video and audio compression technologies, custom micro-controllers and other application specific memories.

Chips, or integrated circuits, begin life in the wafer fabrication "clean room," where several basic processes are repeated to create the many layers that make up the chip's circuitry. Chips are cut out and separated from each other, assembled and then sealed in various plastic packages before undergoing rigorous testing.

MITSUBISHI SEMICONDUCTOR AMERICA, INC.

The skilled hands and innovative minds of MSAI employees are crucial to the company's success, a fact acknowledged and appreciated by management. Additionally, MSAI tries to meet the needs of its employees through various means which include: training for professional and personal development, an ever-changing and challenging work environment, company sponsored employee and family activities, competitive pay and benefits, and on-site recreation facilities.

MSAI also believes in supporting its community. A foundation for corporate philanthropy allows the company to support its primary philanthropic mission—the improvement of local public education. Also high on the list of priorities is corporate support of social services, the arts, and other community activities. An employee volunteer program gives 650 volunteer hours a year to local community organizations that include, among others: museums, highway clean-up projects, boys' and girls' clubs, and the Duke Children's Classic. In addition, MSAI works with the Mistubishi Electric America Foundation to support national foundation activities associated with children with disabilities.

Mistubishi Semiconductor America, Inc. strives to meet the challenge of excellence through quality employees, quality products, and a commitment to outstanding customer service and corporate citizenship. 🗋

Durham's business, insurance and financial communities offer a strong foundation for the area's growing economy.
Photo by Bob Hopkins/Impact Photography.

chapter thirteen
BUSINESS & FINANCE

North Carolina is one of the country's strongest states for banking. And a bank that has been on the scene for virtually this whole century is Central Carolina Bank (CCB).

CENTRAL CAROLINA BANK

CCB has flourished as a result of its legendary commitment to service. The late CCB chairman, George Watts Hill, defined that attitude in 1963 when he said, "There have been many changes in our bank, but only one purpose. That purpose is service—service with geographical definition. We believe in central Carolina and its dynamic expansion and development—an area deserving of a bank that specializes in area needs, that is devoted to the requirements of the people in this area."

CCB, housed in downtown Durham's most familiar and well-loved landmark, the CCB Building, is thriving. CCB's corporate leaders are determined to maintain the friendly, service-oriented excellence of the past while developing a cutting-edge strategy for the financial marketplace.

For more than 90 years, CCB has experienced a steady increase in assets and locations, and today holds an enviable position in the financial market. "We have a balance between consumer and commercial customers that produces a very good mix of business and provides us with an environment of growth," said Ernest C. Roessler, CCB president and chief executive officer. "We did things right in the past, so we have a strong capital base today."

The company is so devoted to its mission of providing excellent customer service, it has adopted an appropriate slogan: "We'll help you find a way." Each employee is trained in the corporation's priorities: customers, employees, the com-

CCB's building is a powerful presence in the Durham skyline.

munities, and the shareholders. Management believes strongly that by serving customers, employees, and their communities well, the shareholders will automatically benefit.

Although the bank has a strong commitment to working with customers in central North Carolina, the boundaries of today's banking service extend beyond Durham. Back in 1990, the CCB Financial Corporation's Board of Directors adopted a strategic plan that called for extending its franchise in the corridor between Raleigh-Durham and Charlotte.

David Woodell, vice president of commercial lending in Durham and Jack McGhee, a local developer and president of Ticon, Inc., look over construction plans at a site in Durham.

The plan served as a road map for CCB's future as a mid-tier bank big enough to compete with North Carolina's megabanks while still retaining a small-town touch to match that of the state's community banks. The plan demanded that CCB operate more efficiently and, for the foreseeable future, independently.

In 1994, the CCBF Board of Directors fine-tuned the strategic plan, focusing on the smooth integration of banks and savings and loans that had become a part of the CCB family.

In its westernmost market of Lenoir, CCB offers commercial services and loan products that were not available before the acquisition of Mutual Savings Bank of Lenoir and Citizens Savings of Lenoir.

After a period of uncertainty, Graham Savings Bank has settled into the CCB family and now provides a vital branch link between the corporate headquarters in Durham and a growing presence in Greensboro.

In Greensboro, 1st Home Federal branches were seamlessly integrated into the CCB operation. Because of superb teamwork of CCB and former 1st Home Federal employees, deposits and loans are up, and the future looks bright as the Triad economy continues to rebound and grow.

And finally, CCB announced recently its largest acquisition ever, signing a definitive agreement to combine with Security Capital Bancorp of Salisbury. The move fulfilled two strategic objectives. First, it colored in CCB's franchise map between the Triad and Charlotte markets. Second, it dramatically increased CCB's presence in the state's largest market.

Adding Security Capital's business to existing CCB deposits in Charlotte catapults CCB from thirteenth to fourth in market share for the Charlotte Metropolitan Statistical Area (MSA). The CCB-Security Capital combination enables CCB to close in on $5 billion in assets.

Roessler says there are no plans to extend beyond the state line. "Not that we're not visionary, but we feel it's better to stay within ourselves," he said. "We'll continue to look for acquisition opportunities in the Piedmont, but we won't force growth. Our franchise has grown as we've reached out into the Piedmont area, but our heart is still in Durham."

CCB executives don't concern themselves with speculation about the future of the state's mid-tier banks, which command 30 percent of the market and are smaller than the multi-state megabanks and larger than the community banks that dot the landscape. Roessler is confident that CCB can compete with the financial power of the multi-state banks and the finesse of the community institutions.

"As a mid-tier bank, we believe that we're meeting this challenge by remembering who we are," Roessler added. "We provide the best of both worlds—we're small enough to stay

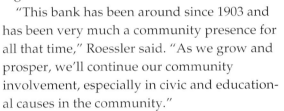

CCB's unique partnership with Lestep Realty, Inc. of Durham provides affordable housing in the community. Maggie Volk, CCB's Durham mortgage lending manager and Levell Exum, president of Lestep, are pictured at a homesite they worked together on for a customer.

close to customers with consistency and continuity, but we're big enough to offer a full array of products and services."

The excellent service theme carries over to administrative duties at CCB as well as to individual employees who take seriously their commitment to the community in which they live. The bank encourages active volunteerism, from tutoring math to coaching soccer.

"This bank has been around since 1903 and has been very much a community presence for all that time," Roessler said. "As we grow and prosper, we'll continue our community involvement, especially in civic and educational causes in the community."

CCB remains an integral part in the growth, development, and quality of life in its communities. In 1994, CCB donated a half- million dollars to 25 community organizations in Alamance County ranging from the local hospice to the volunteer fire department. CCB demonstrates its commitment to the community in seven school districts where the bank sponsors the Gold Star Teacher of the Year program.

CCB has weathered some profound changes in the past decade on its journey to becoming one of the state's financial powerhouses. In that time, it hasn't lost the personal manner that engendered success in the first place. The bank stands ready to confront the challenge of serving customers, communities, and shareholders into the 21st century.

"One advantage that CCB will continue to enjoy," Roessler said, "is that we never forget who we are—a community bank with the financial services that our changing world demands and our customers need." ⧉

William L. Burns, Jr., Chairman of the Board and Ernest C. Rossler, President and Chief Executive Officer.

Since its founding in 1898, the North Carolina Mutual Life Insurance Company has grown to become one of Durham's most wide-

NORTH CAROLINA MUTUAL LIFE INSURANCE COMPANY

ly known and successful business institutions.

With assets of more than $228 million and nearly $10 billion of insurance in force, North Carolina Mutual (NCM) is the nation's largest black life insurance company and ranks among the top 10 percent of all the life insurance companies in the United States.

NCM is licensed to operate in 21 states and the District of Columbia and has offices in 11 states and Washington, D.C. The company's heartbeat and operational center is its beautiful home office building in downtown Durham, atop the highest hill in the city.

But it hasn't always been this way. In fact, the company had a rocky start. Its seven founders included some of the area's most prominent black professionals of the day. John Merrick, the organizer and NCM's first president, was Durham's leading black entrepreneur. He owned a string of barber shops, had substantial real estate holdings, and helped organize a black fraternal insurance society.

The Mutual's other founders included Dr. Aaron M. Moore, Durham's first black physician, who would become the company's second president; Dr. James E. Shepard, a pharmacist and educator, who would later found what is now North Carolina Central University; and William G. Pearson, a business associate of Merrick's and president of the fraternal insurance society.

An early financial crisis tested the resolve of the seven founders, with five of the men dissolving their relationship with the company. John Merrick and Dr. Moore remained, and the company was able to survive the difficult early years largely on the grit, determination, and resources of these two men.

Merrick and Moore reorganized the company in 1900 and brought in C.C. Spaulding, Dr. Moore's nephew, to help lead it into the future.

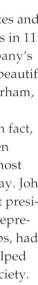

The company's senior officers : (seated) Bert Collins, President and CEO, and (standing L-R) Charles Welch, Vice President-Agency Director; James Parrish, Executive Vice President; and Charles Blackmon, Senior Vice President. (Not pictured: Willie Closs, Jr., Senior Vice President-Controller).

Mutual Plaza, North Carolina Mutual's Home Office Building in Downtown Durham.

Spaulding, who became NCM's third president, steered North Carolina Mutual into a company with a national base. Under his leadership, the company expanded throughout the Southeast and into major metropolitan areas in the Midwest and Northeast.

But North Carolina Mutual never abandoned or overlooked its home base—Durham and North Carolina. Since its organization, the company has had a strong philanthropic attachment to the Durham black community. This attitude was rooted in the philosophies of racial self-help and uplift which had been promoted by Booker T. Washington and which found favor with John Merrick and Dr. Moore. The phrase, "Merciful to all," was the company's first motto.

Thus, with an innate corporate social conscience, the company formulated its concept of the "Double-Duty Dollar." This concept was based on the premise that income from insurance premiums could be reinvested back into the black community through jobs, investments, loans, contributions, and mortgages for the establishment of homes, businesses, churches, and educational institutions. Moreover, it was Merrick's view that the company could provide a strong base for the development of black families, by providing jobs and opportunities for a struggling black population.

As the company grew, it began to be looked upon as a symbol of black entrepreneurial success. In reality, it was much more than that. Because of the vision and spirit of its leaders, North Carolina Mutual spawned and was the economic and inspirational force behind the development of other successful black businesses in Durham, as well. Mechanics and Farmers Bank, the Mutual Community Savings Bank, and NCM Capital Management, Inc.—all ranked among the nation's largest black financial institutions—can trace their beginnings to North Carolina Mutual.

But the symbolism attached to the success of North Carolina Mutual was also important, and Parrish Street, on which NCM and other black financial institutions were located, became known as "The Black Wall Street of America." Many national and international figures have made the offices of North Carolina Mutual a "must-see" place during their visits to Durham. Eleanor Roosevelt, Vice President Hubert H. Humphrey, governors, foreign ambassadors, and scores of sports and entertainment stars have visited the company through the years.

Long before they became established fixtures in the American workplace, women were a part of the North Carolina Mutual story. From the beginning, the role of women has been an important one in the growth and success of the company. That tradition continues today as women serve on the company's board of directors and hold top executive, managerial, and supervisory positions.

For years, North Carolina Mutual has had a reputation as being a great place to work and offers job opportunities in 50 different occupational areas. The company currently has over 600 employees at its Durham headquarters and sales office locations. Because of its history of stressing education and offering career opportunities for its employees, a national publication recently listed NCM as one of the "50 Best Places" in the United States for blacks to work.

Its national reputation as being a great place for young black professionals to grow has helped North Carolina Mutual attract top talent from across the country. The company's annals are filled with names such as John M.

Avery, William J. Kennedy, Jr., George Cox, Viola G. Turner, Asa T. Spaulding, William A. Clement, Maceo A. Sloan, Dr. Charles Watts, and James N. Parrish—all of whom were recruited to Durham by North Carolina Mutual.

That these people not only became leaders of the company but also leaders in the Durham community is a strong testament of the company's ongoing commitment to corporate citizenship and community service.

Bert Collins, NCM's current president, fits that mold perfectly. A native of Texas, Collins was recruited to NCM while living in Detroit and preparing for his CPA examinations. Working his way through a series of administrative and executive positions, he was named NCM's eighth president in July, 1990.

Continuing the company's long-standing tradition of active leaders, Collins is a member of the board of the Public Service Company of N.C. and has served as chairman of the Raleigh-Durham International Airport Authority and as chairman of the board of trustees of North Carolina Central University. Currently, he is also vice chairman of the board of Mutual Community Savings Bank and a board member of Wachovia Bank. In July, 1994, he was elected president of the National Insurance Association, the trade organization of the black life insurance industry.

Collins recently unveiled his "Five Point" vision plan for the company's future: *Be excellent in everything we do. Give the best service we can to our policyholders. Grow, expand, and be competitive. Be profitable. Maintain excellent management.*

Excellence in management and service, growth and profitability, and a strong commitment to community service have been the underpinnings of the company's basic philosophy for nearly 100 years. From this foundation, the company—and Durham—have been served well.

Bert Collins intends to see that this philosophy, and his vision, extend far into the 21st century.

Other top officers include (seated) Theresa Lyons, Vice President-Corporate Secretary; and (standing, L-R) Edward Bowser, Vice President-Information Services; Gregory Fitzmaurice, Vice President-Chief Actuary; and Keith Corbett, Vice President-Treasurer.

DURHAM CHAMBER OF COMMERCE

Virtually every person in Durham today—whether they realize it or not—is touched by the Greater Durham Chamber of Commerce. The influence may be simple: a student earns a Chamber-sponsored Honor Card for perfect attendance. It may be profound: a microchip assembler gains a job because of the Chamber's economic development efforts. Or, it may be life-changing: a single mother gets off the welfare rolls and into training school, thanks to the Chamber's JOBS program. This vibrant, progressive organization, now 3,000 members strong, has played a vital role in Durham's development and expansion for more than 100 years.

Its origins date back to 1884, an era when industry was Durham's centerpiece and industrial leaders guided the destiny of the growing town. It was George Washington Watts, a partner in the Duke tobacco venture, who pulled together a coalition of business leaders, dubbed it the Commonwealth Club, and set about working for Durham's greater good. Commonwealth Club members were charged with attracting new industry, adding more railroads, and polishing Durham's image. The club's first coup came in 1888, when it secured Durham's first telephone service. As the Commonwealth Club evolved to become Durham's Chamber of Commerce, it emerged as a strong influence on the life of the community—often at the forefront of current issues and events. It led the push for Durham's first school playgrounds, fought to overhaul city government, and admitted women to its ranks the year before women's suffrage. Durham was the first Chamber in the state to actively involve minorities in its committees and on its Board. It was one of the first Chambers in the country to have a minority president. The Durham Chamber has set an excellent example in human relations.

Today, although the details differ, the issues before the Greater Durham Chamber of Commerce are remarkably similar to those of the Commonwealth Club: public education, transportation, government, economic development—and polishing Durham's image. The official mission statement of the Chamber states its dedication to the "economic well-being of Durham and Durham County," its desire to be a "constructive advocate on public policy issues," and its support of other endeavors that "contribute importantly to the quality of life of the greater Durham community."

Under the leadership of President/CEO Robert H. Booth since 1965, the Greater Durham Chamber of Commerce has remained an influential voice. "The Chamber is in the business of helping business," said Booth. "And business is at the core of what Durham is today—home to Research Triangle Park, a leader in research and development, the City of Medicine. We realize that what is good for Durham is good for business. That's why our members are involved in such a variety of programs, like public education and fighting crime. Over the years, I've found that Chamber members are Durham's staunchest supporters; they really care about this community."

The collective strength of Chamber members has established dozens of innovative programs: Center for a Drug Free Workplace, EDUCATION: TOP PRIORITY, the Durham Workforce Preparedness Initiative, and the City of Medicine initiative. The Chamber spearheaded the effort that won the N.C. School of Science and Mathematics for Durham over strong statewide competition. It was the Chamber that convinced the Durham County Commissioners to impose a room tax and establish a Convention and Visitors Bureau. And it was the Chamber that founded Downtown Durham, Inc. to concentrate on making Downtown Durham a more lively, appealing place. The Chamber membership has even helped move mountains—or at least a pitcher's mound. Chamber support was instrumental in the fight to keep the Durham Bulls in Durham by building a new minor-league baseball stadium downtown.

Naturally, the primary thrust of the Chamber's activities is economic development. The Chamber is credited with attracting tens of thousands of new jobs and more than 1 billion investment dollars to Durham and Durham County. Professionally produced videos about Durham and strong recruitment efforts are supplemented with funds from the New Durham II initiative. This Chamber-driven project targets economic development, public education, Durham's image, crime-fighting, and regional cooperation. "I'm proud of the Chamber's record of success in industry recruitment, and I'm proud we have never recruited any kind of business or industry that would pollute our environment," Booth said.

The Greater Durham Chamber of Commerce (DCC) was one of the founding members of the Raleigh-Durham Regional Association, a cooperative of the Triangle's economic leaders created to market the entire region. Now expanded and called the Research Triangle Regional Partnership, the organization continues to depend on the leadership of the Durham Chamber. Other regional programs such as "Buy Local" also enjoy Chamber support.

One of the Chamber's primary functions is to bring business-people together for networking. "Business After Hours" mixers are held regularly in member locations that range from nursing homes to the Durham Bulls baseball park. "For Members Only" offers monthly breakfast meetings on topics of timely interest. The Durham Chamber Golf Classic and Sponsors Tournament are booked to capacity every year at Treyburn Country Club. MarketPlace is an annual trade show that offers a full day of exhibits, seminars, and fun. Industry Visitation provides a small-group glimpse of Durham's companies and new businesses. And the Chamber's annual meeting is a favorite gathering place for Durham's business leaders.

Small businesses constitute 80 percent of the DCC ranks, so it is no surprise that the Chamber has a thriving Small Business Council. The energetic council initiated the Tabletop Trade Show, a scaled-down version of MarketPlace. Financing options for small businesses fall under the purvey of the Capital Committee. "Small Businessperson of the Year" awards are made at an annual breakfast meeting. And regular meetings of Executive Dialogue offer opportunities for business owners to share common challenges. There are also groups for managers and sales executives.

Although it has a high profile nationally, many people do not realize that the City of Medicine program was born and bred by the Greater Durham Chamber of Commerce. The City of Medicine program is housed separately but is a thriving division of the Chamber,

sponsoring the annual City of Medicine Awards, community health fairs, the Business-Medical Coalition, and the City of Medicine High School Awards. City of Medicine Ambassadors "spread the good news" about Durham's medical assets throughout the world.

The newest component of the Chamber's Health Affairs Division is the Center for a Drug Free Workplace. Like the City of Medicine, it is an off-site Chamber affiliate. For a modest membership fee, employers gain access to drug abuse education, reduced-fee drug testing, and treatment referrals for employees.

The Chamber is also active in the legislative arena, working for legislation that is in the best interest of business and the community.

The Greater Durham Chamber of Commerce sponsors a variety of annual programs that spotlight Durham's leaders. The Athena Award honors a top female businessperson; Leadership Durham prepares two dozen of Durham's up-and-coming leaders for civic responsibilities; the Quality Customer Service Awards highlight excellent customer service; and the prestigious Civic Honor Award which recognizes long term support and involvement in community activities.

Today's Greater Durham Chamber of Commerce not only offers its members an incredible array of services and opportunities, it is a backbone of the Durham community. "Chamber members have shaped Durham's past and will guide its future," said Booth. "We are proud to support Durham."

Mutual Community Savings Bank, SSB spent the early 1990s shedding its time-honored image as a slow, steady growth company

MUTUAL COMMUNITY SAVINGS BANK, SSB

by jumping into today's banking action with both feet. It established its first branch, expanded into Greensboro, evolved from a mutual savings and loan association to become a mutual savings bank, sold stock, increased its assets, and signed a letter of intent to acquire another Greensboro bank. So much for slow, steady growth!

"Our organization has undergone some major changes in the last five years and has made multiple, major transactions from a corporate standpoint," said Mutual President, George K. Quick. "Now we're going to put that behind us. We're interested in getting to the point of concentrating on the immediate business of the day and getting the organization to perform."

The bank was organized in January, 1921, by R.L. McDougald—with about $425 in assets. As Mutual Building and Loan Association, it operated out of one window in Mechanics and Farmers Bank until it moved to 112 West Parrish Street in 1948.

The minority-managed savings bank is now located on East Chapel Hill Street, and the bank's original goal—to provide an institution for depositors to save and get home loans—

The Mutual Executive Team: F.V. "Pete" Allison, Jr., Chairman & Chief Executive Officer; George K. Quick, President/Chief Operating Officer; Leon C. White, Executive Vice President/Chief Financial Officer; Denise R. Brandon, Vice President/Corporate Secretary. Photography by Bill Flemming Design & Photography

continues to be reflected in the current mission statement: ". . . being faithful to our heritage of efficiently and courteously meeting the financial needs of people across all economic and social segments in the communities we serve."

Although the bank has concentrated on providing home loans to Durham's minority community, serving the entire community is important to Mutual Community Savings Bank, SSB. Chairman and Chief Executive Officer F.V. Allison, Jr. said the bank plays a major leadership role, not only in the African-American community in Durham but in the entire Durham community as well.

"Our officers, directors, and members have served in most of the community organizations in the black community and the community as a whole," he said. "And our diverse board of directors is an unselfish group that works totally for the betterment of this organization and the community."

The early 1990s were an opportune time to alter Mutual Community's image as a small, traditional bank that dealt only in mortgage lending and savings deposits. The bank had earned high ratings for excellent performance and for being one of the safest, most creditworthy thrifts in the country.

The decade dawned with the opening of the bank's first branch office on Fayetteville Road. Later that year, a merger agreement with American Federal Savings and Loan Association of Greensboro was completed. At the end of 1992, the corporation converted from a chartered savings and loan association to a chartered savings bank and the bank's name was changed to Mutual Community Savings Bank, SSB. In 1993, the bank converted to a North Carolina chartered stock savings bank and sold 355,380 shares of its common stock at $10 per share.

Mutual Community Savings Bank, SSB anticipates profitable growth as it approaches the turn of the century. It now holds assets of $52 million, coupled with high capitalization, is a measure of the safety and stability of a financial institution. Mutual Community Savings Bank, SSB will use that capital base to expand and grow even further in the decades to come. *d*

Photography by Bill Flemming Design & Photography

▍From law to accounting, architecture to engineering, advertising and consulting to public relations, Durham's professional firms are recognized leaders in their field. Photo by Paul Liggitt Photography.

chapter fourteen
14
PROFESSIONS

d

▍Principals of Thomas, Knight, Trent, King, and Company (from left to right) Seated: Lucy L. Gallo, Stephen E. Hancock, Hubert O. Teer, Jr. Standing: Daniel H. Craig, E.C. Yarborough, H. Lowell Oakley, Jr.

When a major health care provider client of Newsom, Graham, Hedrick & Kennon, P.A. telephoned inquiring about electronic commu-

NEWSOM, GRAHAM, HEDRICK & KENNON, P.A.

nications access directly to their attorney, the response was a quick "we'll arrange it." With state of the art technology already in place, the firm moved quickly to facilitate the appropriate electronic communications platform to its computer system. The firm provides its clients with a unique blend of traditional legal services with modern innovations and convenience.

Newsom, Graham, Hedrick & Kennon, P.A. recently celebrated its centennial year, making it not only the largest law firm in Durham, but also one of the oldest in North Carolina. With 21 attorneys, it also holds the distinction of being the largest law firm headquartered in Durham.

The key to the firm's longevity is simple, according to one of the senior principals, James T. Hedrick. "We're a local firm with mostly local people, but with a regional outlook," he said. The firm's attorneys have diverse backgrounds and educations and are licensed to practice law in states across the country. "The people are what make Newsom, Graham special," said Hedrick.

The firm's law practice and client base are both diverse. Newsom, Graham, Hedrick & Kennon, P.A. serves Fortune 500 and other large corporations, as well as universities, governmental entities, non-profit organizations, small businesses and individuals.

Service to its hometown is, and always has been, important to the firm. "We give back to the Durham community, because it has given us so much," Hedrick said. "We all have a civic conciousness to improve Durham and the Triangle area. We involve ourselves in as many community activities as time will permit."

The firm is divided into three general practice groups—business, litigation and real estate. Specialty areas within that framework include taxation, exempt-organizations, corporations and partnerships, estate planning and administration, securities, environmental, computer law, intellectual property, employment, constitutional, health care and medical liability, municipal, and media law. Regardless of their specialty, however, the firm's attorneys take a team approach to client service. Effectiveness and efficiency are always the highest priorities.

To better serve its clients, the firm is constantly evaluating new practice areas. "We're currently well-suited to meet the needs of our clientele," Hedrick said. "But Durham and the Triangle are rapidly changing, and this is one of the fastest growing areas in the country. There are more and more people coming here to live and do business, and we're very much attuned to that. The firm is, and always has been, well-situated to meet the demands of the future."

The firm was founded in 1890 and the firm's grand traditions continue to this day, as James L. Newsom and A.H. Graham, Jr. continue their law practices with the firm in an "of counsel" capacity. It is the special combination of tradition coupled with innovation that allows Newsom, Graham, Hedrick & Kennon, P.A. to so ably serve its clients and community.

▋ The Attorneys of Newsom, Graham, Hedrick & Kennon, P.A.

Spring Hill is a beautiful example of a planned community containing single-family homes, townhomes, and apartments.

In a world that often touts bigger as better, Duane K. Stewart and Associates, Inc. is a civil engineering firm that chooses to stay small. For the company's clients, that decision means personalized attention.

"We go out of our way to deliver whatever the client needs on the client's time schedule," Duane K. Stewart said. "We strive to give each client prompt, quality service."

Stewart, president and principal engineer for the firm, said such attentive service is possible because employees are willing to go the extra mile to deliver a satisfactory product. "We're involved with projects for individual homeowners, which might require a visit of a couple of hours, as well as projects involving development of major parcels of land which might last several years. They all receive the same quality of work, and we pay the same attention to all projects, regardless of size." Stewart added, "In everything we do, we try to become an extension of the client and respect that client's needs."

Duane K. Stewart and Associates, Inc. (DKSA) was founded in 1979 when the Greensboro native and Virginia Polytechnic Institute graduate turned his entrepreneurial sights on Durham. The firm has designed projects throughout North Carolina, but does the bulk of its work in the Triangle area.

DKSA provides professional services in civil, sanitary, and environmental engineering to private, municipal, commercial, and industrial clients. Those services include feasibility studies, land planning, site plans, street design, and parking facility design. The firm also provides soil and erosion plans, grading plans, water and sewer design, and storm drainage plans.

DKSA has been involved with more than 100 subdivisions in the Durham area, including Marydell, Surrey Green, Spring Hill, Bent Creek, Sunningdale, Vanderidge, and

Waterford. The company was part of the design team that earned a Triangle J Council of Government award in 1987 for Park 40 Plaza, an office complex, and again in 1989 for Crystal Meadows, a multi-family subdivision.

DUANE K. STEWART & ASSOCIATES, INC.

In 1985, DKSA founded a sister company, Triangle Surveyors, Inc. Ronald D. Carpenter, a registered land surveyor, manages the surveying company to provide all phases of surveying including individual lot surveys for loan closings, boundary and topographical surveys, and stakeout for construction.

Much of the Triangle's dense clay soil is unsuitable for traditional septic tanks, so DKSA is often called on to provide alternative wastewater treatment. The company designed the first major low-pressure sewer system for a North Carolina coastal site that the N.C. Department of Health approved. Jeffery H. Lecky, a company project engineer, serves on the N.C. board that establishes state guidelines for low-pressure systems.

Although the tremendous growth in Durham in the 16 years since the company was founded has been good for business, DKSA is cautious about the environmental impact of such development. The company is sensitive to such issues as storm water management, conservation of green space, and wetland preservation. "Durham is our home," Stewart states, "and we want to see it grow with care. Many of our employees have long-standing ties to this part of North Carolina, so we've got a real commitment to our communities. We're proud of our area and plan to be here for the long haul," he remarked. "It continues to be very exciting for us to be part of its growth."

Duane K. Stewart and Jeffery Lecky inspecting a job site.

When E.K. Powe began practicing law in 1950, a Durham law firm with half a dozen members was considered large, and individual

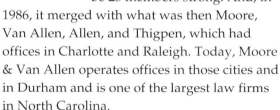

lawyers practiced many areas of law. Today, his law firm, Moore & Van Allen, PLLC, has approximately 135 attorneys in three cities, and the practice of law has become highly specialized.

"Back then, in 1950, Durham was a relatively small, slow-paced community," Powe said. "The major (law) practice areas were automobile accident litigation, workmen's compensation, domestic relations, wills and trusts, residential real estate, and small business practice."

Powe's one-man law firm began to grow when he took on an associate in 1960 and later formed a partnership. Between 1960 and 1986, the firm grew to be 23 members strong. And, in 1986, it merged with what was then Moore, Van Allen, Allen, and Thigpen, which had offices in Charlotte and Raleigh. Today, Moore & Van Allen operates offices in those cities and in Durham and is one of the largest law firms in North Carolina.

▍ E.K. Powe, founding member of Moore & Van Allen's Durham office.

"The biggest impact on the firm in Durham, and one that set the stage for its growth, was the advent of the Research Triangle Park," Powe said. "It brought about a significant change in the economy, moving it from an industrial and rural economy to a high-tech and research-oriented economy and this had a direct influence on specialization in the firm."

The growth of the area's economy caused the law firm to develop a more extensive practice that today includes commercial real estate law; securities law; complicated estate planning and tax law; contract and surety law; health care law; sophisticated finance, banking, transactional and merger and acquisition law; complex business litigation; antitrust law; and intellectual property and patent law.

"We have a strong section in the firm for the latter, which is a direct result of the need arising from the Research Triangle Park," Powe

said. "And we're keenly aware that new technologies have given rise to new areas of practice, which we're constantly pursuing."

While many of the firm's attorneys are native North Carolinians, others come from 30 states and three foreign countries. The recruiting process places emphasis on undergraduate and law school academic achievement, and the firm believes this emphasis provides the greatest assurance that new recruits will excel in the firm's practice groups. Several of Moore & Van Allen's lawyers have scientific backgrounds.

The firm's partners have been active in various civic and community endeavors and have served on boards of charitable, civic, and religious institutions and organizations. They have also been involved in political campaigns and neighborhood groups.

"And the firm encourages lawyers to be involved, as both students and teachers, in further law-related education," Powe said. "They also do extracurricular work, such as pro bono legal work for indigents."

Although the three Moore & Van Allen offices in Durham, Raleigh, and Charlotte operate autonomously, they also operate in support of one another. "The result," Powe said, "is a depth of expertise that one office practicing alone wouldn't have."

"We provide prompt legal services of the highest quality possible," Powe said. "And we've always tried to be creative in solving our clients' problems."

▍ Photography by Bill Fleming Design & Photography

Dick Nelson, Diane Linfors, and Lee Pollard emphasize a full service approach to meeting their clients' needs. Photo by Paul Liggitt Photography.

Nelson & Company is an energetic and forward thinking certified public accounting firm operating from their offices located on University Drive in Durham and Lake Boone Trail in Raleigh. These locations afford easy access to the firm's Triangle market as well as its many out-of-town clients.

The clients of the firm are served by a companywide mission of providing accurate, conscientious accounting and consulting services. Nelson & Company prides itself on providing full-service accounting and consulting, as well as assistance, to clients by planning for the future. The firm has always been proactive in meeting the needs of its clients for audits, reviews, compilations, tax planning, and business planning services. This full-service approach to the client is enhanced by the company's dedication to a team approach to each accounting and consulting engagement.

Dick Nelson and Diane Linfors founded Nelson & Company in the fall of 1983. As business grew, a third partner, Lee Pollard, joined the firm. Soon the initial staff of five expanded into twenty. This growth led to expansion into the University Drive location and a satellite office in North Raleigh.

Not only does Nelson & Company perform top-notch accounting and consulting services, the firm prepares individual, partnership and corporate income tax returns, and estate and trust returns. The firm has computerized all of its operations and is proud of its ability to offer top computer consulting services to its clients. The Nelson & Company client list is a cross section of individuals and companies including manufacturers, retail businesses, profes-

sional service firms, real estate partnerships, construction businesses, not-for-profit companies and foundations, and trusts. The company also provides business and tax consulting for a broad spectrum of businesses.

Nelson & Company offers a high level of accounting services and has its accounting and auditing program reviewed every three years. Under the peer review program conducted by the North Carolina Association of Certified Public Accountants, and the American Institute of Certified Public Accountants, the company has earned the highest possible report each time it has been reviewed. In 1993, the association also honored the firm's dedication to quality and service by presenting the Raymond Rains Outstanding Service Award to Dick Nelson for his years of service to the Association including his work with the implementation of the state wide peer review program.

The Nelson & Company partners strongly believe that their firm should be involved in the community. The firm members actively serve as officers and board directors in many local organizations. In addition, the partners of the firm have participated in the North Carolina Association of Certified Public Accountants as board members and committee members. They have also participated actively in the local Triangle Chapter of this organization. The firm teaches a not-for-profit course through Duke's Continuing Education program, as well as speaking at various civic functions. Nelson & Company tries to make sure that every staff member is involved in some aspect of community service. There is a strong emphasis on the importance of giving something back to the community that has enabled the firm to grow and prosper.

The future looks bright for Nelson & Company as it expands its client base in the Triangle area and beyond. Nelson & Company clients, both inside and outside of North Carolina, can be assured of one very important thing—they'll receive the very best in accounting and consulting services.

KNOTT & ROBERTS ENGINEERING ASSOCIATES, P.A.

A small-firm atmosphere, personal service, high standards, and excellent quality are what clients have come to expect from Knott & Roberts Engineering Associates, P.A. As a direct result, the company is one of the best known and most highly respected consulting engineering firms in the state.

Knott & Roberts was established in 1975, as a two-man office offering mechanical and electrical engineering services for owners and architects in the Triangle area. Today, staff in the firm's offices off I-85 in Durham serve clients throughout North Carolina and in several southeastern cities.

Knott & Roberts takes pride in the high standard of care and quality of work given to more than 140 projects a year, which range in cost from $25,000 to $30 million. The firm has earned a reputation in the engineering industry for producing quality plans and accurate specifications, which translates to the lowest possible bids on construction work.

That 2-man office has grown to a 28-member staff, 7 of whom are professional engineers and 2 engineering graduates. Knott & Roberts' professional engineers have an average of 22 years experience behind them, providing an even greater degree of reliability. The principals at Knott & Roberts Engineering Associates are C. Franklin Knott, Jr., Stancil B. Roberts, John Dale Benson, and Keith M. Spring.

Although Knott & Roberts has seen growth, both in the size of the firm and in the number and size of its projects, the company is determined to maintain its small-business, personal-service atmosphere. Clients work directly with principals, who have a vested interest in customer satisfaction and quality service. The same professionals who design a given project always follow up with regular field inspections during construction.

■ VAMC - Clinical Addition, Durham.

Knott & Roberts has provided engineering and consulting services for a wide variety of projects including: Western Wake Medical Center, Cary; the Durham Bulls Baseball Park; the Duke University Terry Sanford Institute for Public Policy; Hillside Model High School, Durham; the Central Carolina Bank Computer Operations Center; the Clinical Addition to the Durham VA Medical Center; and the Desert Pavilion at the North Carolina Zoo, Asheboro.

Specific design services offered by Knott & Roberts include central heating and air-conditioning systems; building plumbing systems; fire protection; outdoor water and sewer systems; building electrical systems; and outdoor lighting. These services are provided for clients in industry, commerce, education, medicine, governmental agencies, and architectural firms.

The entire engineering industry changes constantly. New and important information arrives daily on materials, codes, energy considerations, and environmental concerns. Knott & Roberts keeps abreast of these changes through seminars, continuing education, and professional associations. The company is fully computerized, using state-of-the-art, computer aided drafting (CAD) systems, although the ever present drafting board is still used occasionally.

About 70 percent of the firm's business is repeat business, and several clients have remained loyal to the firm since the day it opened 20 years ago. There's only one way to explain that kind of devotion—trust. Clearly, Knott & Roberts Engineering Associates' clients depend on the firm to solve engineering problems with an eye on keeping costs down and quality high. *d*

■ Duke University - Terry Sanford Institute for Public Policy.

West & Vaughan puts a lot of stock in partnerships; the firm is actively involved in its clients' marketing efforts, and in turn encourages clients to participate in the creative process. The result is success in the marketplace, for both West & Vaughan and its clients.

"Part of the way we do business is to form partnerships with our clients and involve them in the communications process," says Bill West, president and creative director. Apparently, clients appreciate the joint effort, as evidenced by the exponential growth of the company. When it was founded in 1985, West & Vaughan had one account and $250,000 in billings. Ten years later, annual billings exceeded $25 million.

The company's services are extensive and varied, ranging from traditional communications tools such as print and broadcast advertising, public relations and direct marketing, to more specialized services like lifestyle marketing and customer retention programs.

To further boost the effectiveness of its efforts, the agency has established marketing plans groups within the firm. These groups, comprised of members of the account service staff, the media department and the creative department, hold regular "think tank" brainstorming sessions on behalf of agency clients. "Obviously, we want to deliver a good creative product," West says. "But we also work to be creative on strategic issues. And that means employing creative thinkers across all agency disciplines."

West & Vaughan's broad-based creativity has caught the eye of a wide variety of clients, in both the business-to-business and consumer arenas, who produce products ranging from candy to auto parts. "We feel that diversity, in our client list and in our experience, is a real strength," Executive Vice-President Tom Vaughan says. "Not being focused on one industry is healthy, both creatively and strategically."

The 30 employees at West & Vaughan collectively offer a wealth of advertising and marketing experience. Tom Vaughan's marketing programs for St. Pauli Girl Beer, for example, propelled it from an obscure brand to the number three imported beer in the United States. And Bill West honed his skills in advertising agencies in New York City, Atlanta, and San Antonio, and has put his creative stamp on products as diverse as McDonald's, Delta Airlines, Pet Dairy Products, and Spray 'N Wash.

"Our national experience is always a door opener, because several of us have worked at major agencies and on major accounts," Vaughan said. "But the conversation usually turns pretty quickly to what we're doing now. One of our strongest sales tools is to get a potential client to call an existing client. If that happens, we have a good shot at the business."

Clearly the hallmark of West & Vaughan's company-client relationship is mutual respect and trust, the basis of any successful partnership.

And for West, a Durham native, conducting business in his hometown is an added benefit. When he left North Carolina for Madison Avenue 25 years ago, he never expected to have the opportunity to return. But now his company is earning national awards for national clients—all from a place both partners are proud to call home. 🖉

❚ West & Vaughan Advertising Executive Partners, Bill West and Tom Vaughan.

chapter fifteen
15
BUILDING GREATER DURHAM

HOCK
DEVELOPMENT CORP.
page 140

VANGUARD-ONCOR
INTERNATIONAL
page 141

TEER ASSOCIATES
page 142

d

From the vision to the reality, Durham's development and real estate industry shapes tomorrow's skyline and neighborhoods. Photo by Paul Liggitt Photography.

HOCK DEVELOPMENT CORP.

Slightly more than a decade ago, Gary Hock, president of Hock Development Corp., surveyed a 250-acre tract of former farmland near Durham Regional Hospital and envisioned the future: a mixed use development anchored by medical office buildings with commercial amenities, private accomodations, a child care center, lush landscaping accented by a sparkling lake and preservation of the historic house located on the site.

Today, that same tract of land is known as Independence Park, Raleigh-Durham's preeminent medical office development. Every facet of primary care and nearly every medical specialty is represented within the park's stunning office buildings. Bright Horizons, one of the nation's foremost innovators in child care, occupies a cul-de-sac location deep in Independence Park. The Bonnie Brae house, a vital link to Durham's past, has been restored as the centerpeice for a constellation of townhouses which provide accommodations for health care and corporate users. A bank, a restaurant, and an insurance company share the park, too. A Duke University joint venture initiated a biomedical technology phase of the Park in the mid-1990s; and a senior living phase is in the development stage.

Independence Park is but one of the stellar develoments created by Hock Development Corp. Founded in Pennsylvania by Gary Hock approximately 30 years ago, the firm has built

and developed more than two million square feet of property—primarily Class A office buildings throughout the Southeast, Midwest and Northeast. Now, the firm specializes in build-to-suits with an emphasis on health care-related facilities. The company moved its headquarters to Durham, the City of Medicine, in the early 1980s. Since 1991, Hock has established itself as a leading developer of medical office buildings, primary care facilities, ambulatory care centers, and hospital campus properties. Its rapidly-expanding client list includes subsidiaries of Fortune 500 companies such as Xerox, General Motors, and Columbia/HCA.

The secret to the company's phenomenal success is simple: a personal, hands-on attitude toward each and every project. Company president Gary Hock believes quality lies in the details. All Hock projects start with an in-depth consultation to determine the precise needs of the client. All facets of development—design, engineering, leasing, financing, property management—are coordinated in-house. Turn-key construction is handled by G.M. Hock Construction, Inc. This full service approach allows Hock more control over costs and completion dates, much to the benefit of the firm's clients. The customized formula works: Hock's fine reputation continues to grow regionally and nationally.

Clearly, Hock Development Corp. is a real estate development firm of national caliber. The company is strongly committed to the Durham community, however. Hock's investment in Independence Park is a prime example of the company's support of the local Durham economy. As Hock and Independence Park continue to grow, so will Durham; the future looks bright for all three! ☑

From L to R: Jim Flink, Jerry Levit and Scott Stankavage, principals—Vanguard-ONCOR International.

VANGUARD-ONCOR INTERNATIONAL

In the late 1980s, commercial real estate moved to the forefront as an attractive business investment in the Triangle. With that shift towards institutional ownership came an upsurge in demand for expert property management and brokerage. Thanks to an intimate knowledge of the market, a keen attention to detail, and a unique "no compete" philosophy, Vanguard-ONCOR International quickly emerged as an industry leader.

It was a heady beginning for a company founded in 1987. Principals James T. Flink and Jerome T. Levit originally specialized in site selection and acquisitions for their clients. As the market demanded it, Vanguard stepped in to provide commercial, investment, and industrial real estate brokerage. And as a means of establishing the trust so vital to a solid real estate partnership, Vanguard pledged it would never compete with its clients for properties, either through direct ownership or development.

The combination of Vanguard's unshakable integrity, hard work, and exceptional foresight has produced a company with an impressive array of success stories on behalf of a wide variety of clients. Today, *Vanguard-ONCOR International* stands as one of the top-ranked, independent, full-service commercial real estate firms that serves markets worldwide. Its international presence enhances its importance to major corporations based in the Triangle making Vanguard-ONCOR a formidable, yet approachable heavyweight in the local market.

It was in 1995 that Vanguard was chosen to join ONCOR, one of the oldest and most respected commercial real estate corporations in the world. Vanguard-ONCOR joined 41 other companies that serve 200 markets in 35 countries, securing the multi-market needs of national and multi-national organizations who are locally based.

Based in Durham with offices on Quadrangle Drive and in Raleigh, Vanguard-ONCOR continues to provide unmatched services to the Triangle's commercial real estate community. Vanguard aggressively markets space, negotiates the best possible lease, maintains the physical plant, and stays in touch regularly with owners and tenants alike.

Vanguard views its relationship with clients as a partnership, one that should be mutually beneficial. To that end, Vanguard is organized into teams of managers, agents, and brokers that enable this midsize firm to best serve its growing client base. Vanguard clients know they can depend on expert guidance for brokerage, leasing, property management, consulting, and evaluation services.

The Triangle community depends on Vanguard-ONCOR as a staunch supporter of civic services and events. Vanguard employees serve on boards as diverse as the Chamber of Commerce, the United Way, the Board of Realtors, the Durham YMCA, and the American Cancer Society. It's all in keeping with Vanguard's original concept—to serve the Triangle community and beyond with diligence and professionalism.

Quadrangle Office Park, headquarters of Vanguard-ONCOR International.

TEER
ASSOCIATES

In a tragic 1906 accident, an 18-year-old workman lost his hand while cutting clay into bricks. Rather than bowing to adversity, the young man—Nello L. Teer—set his sights on success, founding a company that would become known around the world. His firm, Nello L. Teer Company, had its roots as a regional company but grew to become a major international contractor.

Today, in his grandfather's footsteps, Robert D. Teer, Jr. is the president of his own company, Teer Associates, a Real Estate Development, Property Management, and Leasing firm. Robb Teer carries on the proud family tradition of perseverance and excellence and applies his grandfather's high ethical standards to his own business.

Nello L. Teer's business ethic served him well. One of the earliest Teer contracts was the site preparation for Duke University's Chapel; others came from an impressive list of public and private institutions. They included work at the University of North Carolina at Chapel Hill, the Blue Ridge Parkway, the

Raleigh/Durham Airport, and the Beaufort, South Carolina, Naval Air Station.

As the company matured in the late 1960s and early 1970s, five third-generation Teers—including Robb Teer—joined Nello L. Teer and his sons, Nello L. Teer, Jr. and R. Dillard Teer, in the family firm. Robb Teer was named Assistant Vice President for Finance and Administration for the firm, a position accountable for work conducted by thousands of people, including international projects in Central America and Africa.

In 1974, the Nello L. Teer Company merged with Romeo Guest Associates, Inc.; six years later, the combined company was sold to Koppers Company. Robb Teer then became Vice President of Teer Enterprises, Ltd. and developed the only commercial and retail space in the Research Triangle Park . This property, when sold in 1985, constituted the largest real estate sale in the history of Durham County at the time. In 1986, Robb formed Teer Associates which has developed approximately 300 acres of commercial property in the Triangle. Its clients include GTE, IBM, Glaxo-Wellcome, the Research Triangle Institute, and NetEdge Systems. Each project, whether a research facility, computer operation center, or executive office, benefits from Teer Associates' years of experience.

Robb Teer has spent more than 25 years in real estate development, management, and leasing. Additionally, he retired in 1994 as a Lieutenant Colonel after serving 27 years with the U.S. Army Reserve. His long service was another lesson firmly instilled by his grandfather's example. "My grandfather was someone who very much believed in giving back to society," he said. The family business Nello L. Teer founded flourished during the evolution of the Triangle from an agrarian-based economy to a high-tech mecca. The Teer name was viewed as strong support for the community, providing a stable job base for hometown citizens.

"I'm excited to be a part of this legacy," Robb Teer said. "My grandfather taught us to conduct business with honesty and integrity, to provide clients with quality and value for a fair price, and to treat everybody as we wanted to be treated." These are qualities reinforced in every Teer Associates transaction today. 𝒹

Robert D. Teer, Jr. in front of the 40,000 sq. ft. NetEdge Systems, Inc. Building completed April 1, 1995.

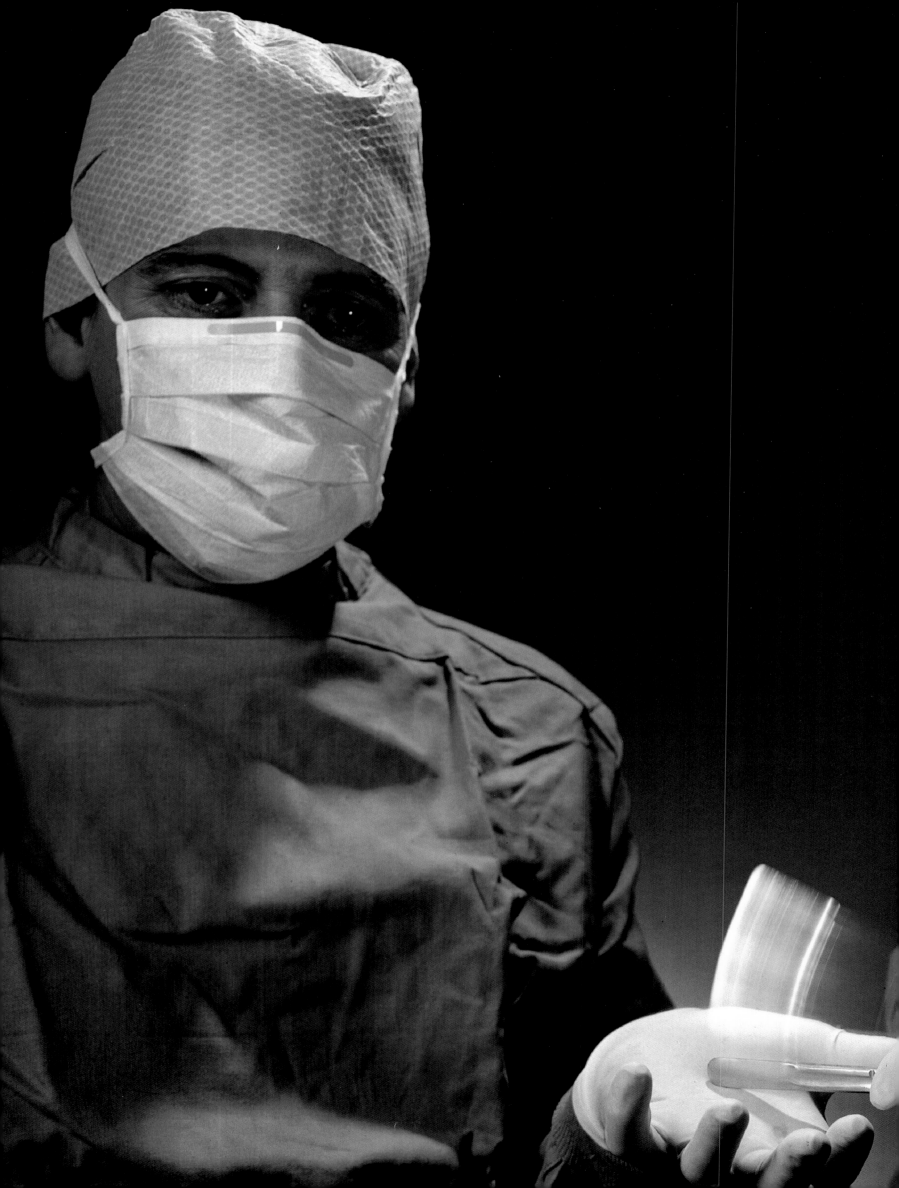

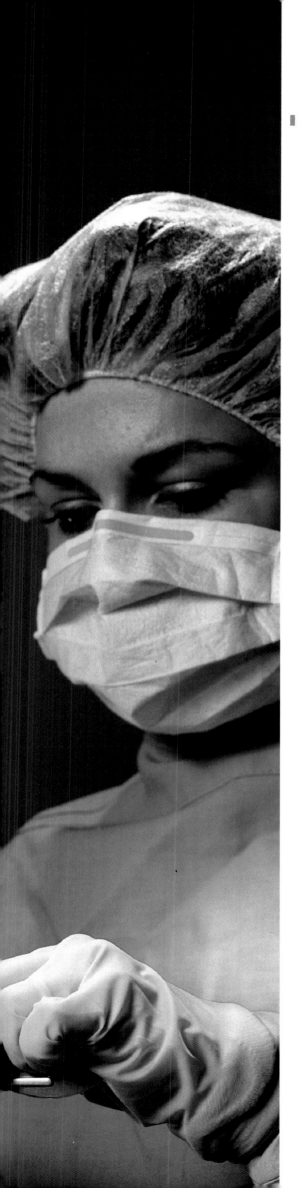

chapter sixteen
16
MEDICINE & EDUCATION

❚ THE MISSION: When Duke University's medical school and hospital opened their doors more than 60 years ago, their broad mission

DUKE UNIVERSITY MEDICAL CENTER

was to educate health professionals, conduct research, and provide patient care. Today, adherence to that mission has positioned Duke University Medical Center as one of the world's leading academic medical centers, poised to play a dominant role as contemporary medicine enters the 21st century.

"We have an extremely high national and international presence, but we're also entrepreneurial and innovative and fast moving on the local front," Chancellor Ralph Snyderman said. "We meet change and provide leadership in a time of change." Duke's adaptability is one reason its medical school has long been recognized as one of the finest in the country. It is consistently ranked as one of the nation's top medical schools; more than 7,000 students vie for one of the 100 spaces that open each year. The medical school attracts students to Durham from North Carolina and across the United States. In today's rapidly changing medical climate, Duke medical students are taught to share their skills in the community, as well as in hospital settings.

"We also train graduate nurses, physical therapists and physicians assistants who work throughout the state, and residents and fellows in specialties of medicine," Snyderman said. "The people we train contribute a lot to the communi-

❚ A renowned biomedical research center, Duke is one of the largest recipients of funding from the National Institutes of Health.

ty through clinics and outreach programs."

Those who train at the medical school are part of a premier research institution that's respected worldwide. The medical center is one of the largest recipients of federal funding for research. That's a vote of confidence from some of the nation's most knowledgeable scientists, who trust Duke University Medical Center to conduct research that will lead to improvements in patient care. "Our research is the source of major discoveries to better understand and treat cancer, heart disease, and Alzheimer's disease," Snyderman said. "This has an important impact both locally and nationally."

As vital as both education and research are, they're the tools that serve a larger mission—the care of patients. Since Duke University Medical Center opened in 1930, it has been a source of hope, healing, and caring for people throughout the Southeast and the nation. Today, there are 600,000 patient visits a year to the medical center's clinics and more than 30,000 hospital admissions. A clinical faculty of more than 1,000, a house staff of 900, and nursing and support staff of 10,000 deliver excellent care in what has become the largest health care facility in the state.

❚ THE VISION: The story of Duke University Medical Center begins with James Buchanan Duke, the youngest son of Durham tobacco merchant Washington Duke. James B. Duke believed that a great university could grow out of Durham's Trinity College, and he made a bold investment that resulted in the creation of the university and the establishment of the $40

❚ Bronze statue of James Buchanan Duke stands watch over the university he endowed.

million Duke Endowment. When he died in 1925, his will directed that $4 million be used to establish a medical school, a hospital, and a nurses' home.

Duke had accurately assessed the need for health care in the Carolinas. At that time, North Carolina was one of the poorest states in the nation, with a shortage of physicians and hospitals. There was no four-year medical school in the state. Duke's bequest changed all that. In 1927, pediatrician Wilburt Cornell Davison was recruited from the Johns Hopkins University School of Medicine in Baltimore to be the first dean of Duke's fledgling medical school. He began to develop a medical curriculum for Duke in the esteemed Johns Hopkins tradition. When the hospital and medical school opened in 1930, the high standards that would be the medical center's hallmark were firmly in place.

Duke's transition from a medical school and hospital to an expanded medical center began shortly after World War II. Basic and applied research, patient care, medical teaching, consulting, and community applications of biomedical knowledge all became part of the medical center's commitment to excellence. New medical concepts and techniques evolved, and federal government funding began to play a more prominent role in biomedical research. By the time Davison retired in 1960, after 33 years as dean, Duke University Medical Center was the preeminent medical center in the southeastern United States.

Under Barnes Woodhall, M.D., dean from 1960 to 1964 and William Anlyan, M.D., dean from 1964 to 1988, a new generation of medical school leadership was recruited. The impact of research on the practice of medicine began to emerge, and new curricula to train physician-researchers was developed. The physical plant expanded, with 13 new clinical and basic research buildings and the North Division of Duke University Hospital. When the dust settled, Duke offered 1,125 beds to patients from all walks of life.

❚*EDUCATION:* Today, Duke University's medical school gleans wisdom from its past as it embraces the future. The high standards of excellence established by Davison are still firmly in place, but in addition, students are exposed to an education unique in the field.

They receive training that combines scholarship in the basic sciences, early clinical experience, individual study, ethics, and the development of human values.

The medical school curriculum prepares students for a lifetime of self-learning. The first year is devoted to gaining a familiarity with the basic sciences; the second year's clinical clerkships take students to patients' bedsides. With a well-grounded knowledge in the basic sciences and patient care, students are then ready for a third year of exploration and research in their particular field of interest. The fourth year is spent in elective clinical clerkships.

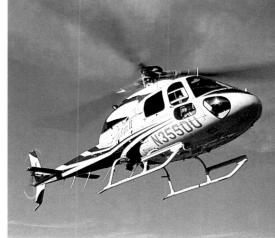

Teaching medical students is just one part of Duke University Medical Center's educational mission. Duke is nationally recognized for its residency and clinical fellowship training programs. A wide range of medical and surgical specialties makes Duke's internships, residencies, and fellowships among the most desirable in the nation.

The Duke Graduate School of Nursing and allied health programs in physical therapy, biometry, and health administration round out the training of the health care team. In addition, the physician's assistant program, established at Duke in 1965, was the first in the country and now serves as a model for 53 other programs at medical centers nationwide.

❚*RESEARCH:* Thanks to state-of-the art biotechnology tools, health care professionals

❚ Flying more then 2,000 missions a year, Duke's Life Flight helicopters are a lifeline to community hospitals throughout North Carolina and surrounding states.

❚ Combining early clinical experiences with scholarship in the basic sciences, a Duke medical education prepares young physicians for a lifetime of self learning.

today uncover answers to incredibly complex clinical questions. High technology has encouraged considerable growth and development in research at Duke University Medical Center. Coupled with research dollars, biotechnology paves the way for curing diseases long thought to be incurable.

A bone marrow transplant program, cancer research, cardiovascular research that's making inroads against heart disease, and research in genetics are just a few of the ways in which research dollars make a difference at Duke University Medical Center. One day, researchers hope to develop diagnostic procedures that detect inherited disease and discover possible therapies that will correct genetic defects. A greater understanding of the brain and nervous system and an emphasis on cell biology also come under the research umbrella.

The application of research to the practice of medicine allows physicians to better understand the basic processes of life and of disease. News-breaking biomedical research discoveries and a vast array of clinical and technological resources combine to benefit Duke patients. Lifesaving innovations developed in Duke's research labs dramatically alter clinical diagnosis and treatment.

These research advances are shared with the medical community through a network of partnerships with physicians and hospitals—locally, nationally, and globally. Community

Formerly the site of Duke Hospital, the Gothic buildings on the original Duke medical campus are now home to Duke's outpatient clinics.

Books, toys, games and play are an important part of the care at Duke Children's Hospital

physicians and hospitals also participate in Duke's clinical trials, research protocols, and education programs. Duke University Medical Center enjoys a good-neighbor relationship with several institutions in the Research Triangle Park. Consequently, research conducted at the medical center finds an avenue for appropriate application and production. "The applications of these discoveries can be quite profound," Snyderman said. "So we try to work with our RTP neighbors on our discoveries, and RTP is known nationwide for its ability to collaborate with Duke."

HEALTH CARE: The Research Triangle area also benefits from having one of the best health care providers in the world in its backyard. A health care facility of Duke's caliber allows patients with complex, difficult-to-treat illnesses to get prompt diagnosis and treatment. Duke is known worldwide for its work in cardiovascular disease, cancer, neurological diseases, and AIDS research. In addition, the medical center is an innovator in the area of endoscopic surgery.

"The advantage to the community of having an academic medical center here is that the local hospital for many residents happens to be one of the best medical centers in the world," Snyderman said. "Individuals come from all over the area and the world, so a community hospital is also an international hospital."

Although academic medical centers have long been known for teaching and research,

Duke University Medical Center is constantly reevaluating its "ivory tower" mission to make sure it has relevance to the community, especially to Durham. That reevaluation has moved the medical center to reconsider use of its hospital facilities. When more than 700 beds were added to the hospital system in 1980-81 with the building of Duke North, the total 1,125 beds filled patient needs. Today, the number of hospital beds at Duke North satisfies the entire inpatient population at the medical center.

"The good practice of medicine doesn't require the hospitalization that was required in 1980, and much can be done in ambulatory facilities," said Snyderman. "So we'll build a state-of-the-art ambulatory surgery center." Ten years ago, many surgeries couldn't be done in an ambulatory outpatient facility, but the days when gallbladder surgery or hernia repair required a 7 to 10-day stay in the hospital are over. Now, advances in instrumentation and medical care shift such procedures from inpatient to outpatient settings and out into the community.

❚ *THE FUTURE:* Moving health care out into the community will become more common in the 21st century, and Duke University Medical Center is already adapting to the changing medical climate. When it became obvious that managed care would be an increasingly vital component of health care, the medical center moved to provide medical services that better serve today's patients. In a partnership new in the medical field, an academic medical center and a for-profit managed-care company joined forces to deliver innovative high quality, low-cost managed care.

Increasingly, health care in the nation is taking place away from the traditional hospital setting. The medical center's satellites for primary and specialty care allow less intensive care to be provided at a facility convenient to the patient, although complex procedures will continue to be performed in the hospital.

"An ideal health care system," according to Snyderman, "is one where people can get in at a level appropriate for them, whether they are basically healthy or have a life-threatening disease. We're a full-service health care provider, but if the health problem is life-threatening, we're the best facility in the world. We're the 24-hour fire station, open all the time."

To best serve the health care needs of the entire community, medical center leaders regularly meet with city council members, county commissioners, minority leaders, the mayor, and the governor to discuss community health care issues. In addition, local universities collaborate with Duke on joint community education efforts.

"We have a national and international presence that benefits the entire region and helps all of us," Snyderman said. "The fact that Duke is here gives a big center of gravity to health care. We're a very large player in the health care arena." ❚

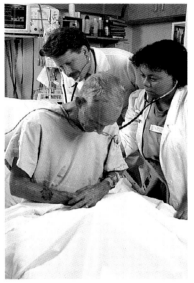

❚ From primary care to the treatment of complex disorders, Duke has long been recognized as one of the world's leading hospitals.

❚ Drawing patients from across the Southeast and the nation, Duke University Hospital has been housed in this sleek and modern facility since 1980.

Duke University Hospital North Division

In today's medical environment, the emphasis has shifted from health care to health. This fundamental change has directly impacted the

DURHAM COUNTY HOSPITAL CORPORATION

focus of the Durham County Hospital Corporation (DCHC), according to President Richard Myers.

"The mission of Durham County Hospital Corporation is to improve the health status of the community," he said.

"The medical community can no longer survive by staying home and fixing things when people come for help. We must interact with the community-at-large; you can't provide health care in a vacuum."

"A true health care system involves decision makers at all levels—both state and local—who set priorities that address a community's specific needs," says Myers. For DCHC, that means taking into account issues such as substance abuse, violence intervention, nutrition, teenage pregnancy, and low birthweight babies. Myers reports an increasing number of health-related problems now revolve around such community issues. Better health for the community can mean healthier, more productive citizens. With an orientation toward wellness, rather than illness, tomorrow's health

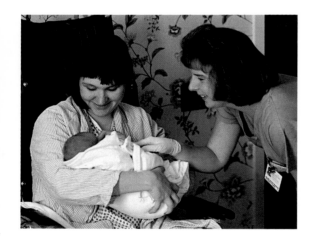

care system in Durham is pointed towards more outpatient and community-based services, like those now offered through DCHC.

Durham County Hospital Corporation was founded in 1971 as a not-for-profit entity, governed by a 15-member Board of Trustees who are appointed by the Durham County Commissioners. The corporation offers Durham a wide array of health options: Durham Regional Hospital, a general and acute-care hospital; Oakleigh, a substance abuse facility; Durham Regional HomeCare, a home health agency; Lincoln Community Health Center, an outpatient clinic; Durham County Emergency Medical Services; Durham Ambulatory Surgical Center; and the Watts School of Nursing. Mindful of its diverse patient population, DCHC continues to devel-

op programs that target specific issues, such as women's health, aging, and home health care.

Acute-care facilities are at the heart of DCHC, with Durham Regional Hospital as its centerpiece. This 451-bed hospital is a community hospital and a regional referral center. As the health care climate changes, Durham Regional has begun to reach out into the community to provide user-friendly services to Durham citizens. "We respond to the needs of the community," said Larry Suitt, senior vice president and chief operating officer of Durham County Hospital Corporation. "We don't determine what those needs are. We allow the community to tell us and we respond."

Durham Regional Hospital, which linked the former Lincoln Hospital and Watts Hospital, opened in 1976. Over the years, several capital improvement projects expanded the physical facilities at the hospital site. In 1994-1995, a major expansion and renovation project improved the hospital's capabilities for emergency and outpatient services, increased operating room capacity, and improved department functioning throughout the hospital. A new 15,000-square-foot building was also constructed for radiation therapy for cancer patients, a joint venture between DCHC and Duke University Health System. The improvements were driven by increasing demands from the citizens Durham Regional serves. "We're not here building monuments to our own success," Suitt said. "We're trying to address the needs of the community and thereby ensure our own success."

Although Durham Regional serves inpatients with the finest medical care, outpatient services have been expanded. Durham Regional's Health Services Center, a comprehensive health delivery facility, offers quality medical services at a reasonable cost with an emphasis on continuity of care. The Center, located on Crutchfield Street, provides "one-stop" health care close to major roads, and is also accessible by public transportation. The Durham Ambulatory Surgical Center offers an outpatient alternative for simple surgical procedures in state-of-the-art facilities near the hospital. For more complicated outpatient surgery, the hospital has its own ambulatory surgery department.

Many of the nurses who staff Durham Regional Hospital and its constellation of outpatient services were trained on campus at the Watts School of Nursing, one of North Carolina's oldest diploma schools. When Watts School of Nursing celebrated its 100-year anniversary in 1995, it was an opportunity to reaffirm its original purpose. "The mission of the school is to train the best possible clinical nurse," said Dr. Peggy Baker, director of nursing education. "Nurses who graduate from Watts have the theoretical and practical perspective that allows them to put theory and knowledge together in a clinical setting."

That commitment to train competent clinical nurses was part of the school's philosophy from the outset. "In those early days,"...the program was very intensive, with a great deal of emphasis placed on clinical training." Those early students, single women between the ages of 23 and 30, took up the challenge of a curriculum that spanned anatomy to medical jurisprudence. Despite the rigors of the program, Ethel Clay became the school's first graduate in 1897. She was followed by a long line of students who established a tradition of excellence at the school. Today's students reflect a more diverse cross section: they come to Watts married or single, male or female, without regard to age. Many of them have chosen second careers in nursing while juggling families, jobs, and community responsibilities. The school tries to accommodate such high-pressure schedules through innovative scheduling and pre-entrance college course requirements.

Since 1895, 2,300 nurses have received diplomas from Watts. Today's average state board passing rate for graduates is higher than 95 percent. The high scores are directly attributable to the exceptional Watts faculty, which is dedicated to the profession of nursing. In the words of one Watts graduate, "I didn't learn how to be a nurse here. I became a nurse here." Faculty members strive to help students and graduates maximize their opportunities. A Watts education provides a clinical program that opens doors to other areas of nursing. Alumnae provide care in a variety of settings and are sought after not only in Durham, the "City of Medicine", but throughout the state and nation.

The dedication of Watts nurses, its emphasis on wellness, and the high-quality care provided through Durham Regional Hospital and its subsidiaries combine to ensure a bright future for Durham County Hospital Corporation. And always, at the core of all its work, is a commitment to the well-being of the Durham community.

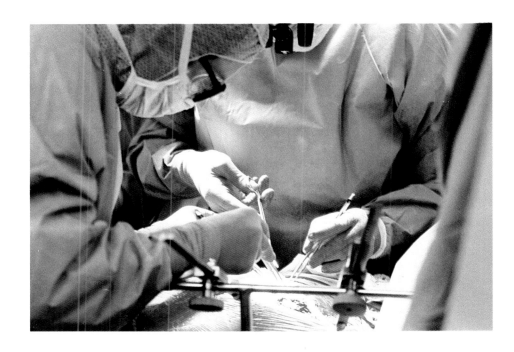

Doctors Health Plan, Inc. is a comprehensive HMO (health maintenance organization) that prides itself on delivering affordable, high-

DOCTORS HEALTH PLAN, INC.

quality medical care through a "user friendly" system. Its goal is to offer medical coverage to employers who want the best possible medical care for their employees.

The company, part of Coastal Physician Group, Inc., is renowned for its innovative approach to managed care. Basic and supplemental services are provided with an eye on quality, efficient use of resources, and cost control. The strengths of Doctors Health Plan

derive in part from the focus of its parent company. Both are North Carolina based. Both see physicians as the integral part of a successful managed-care delivery system. Both recognize the importance of a strong, experienced management team.

Founded in 1977 and headquartered in Durham, Coastal Physician Group, Inc. is the nation's largest physician services company. It employs more than 4,000 people and operates in 46 states. Coastal delivers over 30 percent of hospital-based emergency services across North Carolina.

Doctors Health Plan, which also has its headquarters in Durham, has a distinct advantage in serving the community in which it is based. Not only are the needs of the North Carolina market understood, but physicians and hospitals in this market already do business with Coastal. Consequently, Doctors Health Plan can create products that appeal to North Carolinians and contract with a network of physicians who trust that a physician services company will work with them, not against them.

Coastal established Doctors Health Plan in

1994 in response to the growing need for an outstanding managed-care organization. The plan seeks to improve the health status of North Carolina communities by offering first-class care through a network of primary care physicians, specialists, and ancillary care providers. As the name suggests, Doctors Health Plan carefully considered the opinions of physicians as it developed policies and procedures, product lines, and administrative requirements. With physician input, the company created a plan that is user friendly and attractive to physicians. As a physician company, Doctors Health Plan draws on relationships with the local health-care community in an ongoing cooperative and innovative effort to improve health-care quality for its members.

The management team at Doctors Health Plan consists of a variety of individuals from leading HMOs across the country. Doctors Health Plan is structured on a solid foundation of experience that enables it to build on what works and to improve on what hasn't worked for competing HMOs. In addition to using experience as a guide, Doctors Health Plan uses the National Committee for Quality Assurance guidelines in the creation of all policies and procedures.

Convenient access to local primary care physicians and the option to change physicians at any time are the hallmarks of a health-care plan that puts patients first. Doctors Health Plan emphasizes patient satisfaction. Patients choose their own primary care physician from a group of top-flight doctors who meet the plan's stringent requirements. Physicians accepted by the plan undergo on-site inspections, a quality review, and a biennial credentials check. Physicians manage the care for their Doctors Health Plan patients to ensure accurate, effective treatment. Doctors Health Plan physicians participate in Physician Quality Incentive programs, which reward them for quality of care and quality of service.

Doctors Health Plan, through other subsidiaries of the parent company, offers physicians a variety of value-added services to improve the profitability of their practices. These services include billing, collections, information technology, purchasing, credentialing, liability insurance, and staffing. Together, these features have enabled Doctors

Health Plan to enter the market with a healthy list of participating providers. Doctors Health Plan was the first HMO to sign an agreement with North Carolina Preferred Providers, the PHO (Physicians Hospital Organization) associated with Durham Regional Hospital.

To better meet the medical needs of its members, Doctors Health Plan conducts ongoing research to evaluate treatment methods, health habits, and the underlying causes of disease. The company has found that the most effective treatment to reduce symptoms and produce cures are discovered by measuring outcomes and analyzing results.

And to keep a finger on the membership pulse, random surveys of companies that use Doctors Health Plan measure satisfaction with the plan and help set standards of physician availability and accessibility.

Doctors Health Plan strongly emphasizes wellness and preventive care. An extensive array of services helps members assess and reduce their own health risks. Members receive discounts at fitness and weight loss centers and at sporting goods and nutrition stores. Free self-help information, including a series of booklets on health improvement, gently points employees toward healthier lives. There are also plan-sponsored programs that highlight

fitness, weight control and smoking cessation. Even the prenatal program for expectant mothers has a wellness component: a nurse is available for consultation; the plan charges only one small copayment for the first prenatal visit—the remainder are covered at no charge; and the plan pays for approved prenatal classes so that the next generation of plan members arrive healthy and strong.

Accurate, up-to-date medical information is available on a toll-free hot line, and a quarterly newsletter keeps members informed about health issues. Doctors Health Plan also offers workplace seminars on hypertension, cholesterol control and stress management.

Doctors Health Plan, Inc. is rapidly establishing itself as a leader in the HMO arena and will continue to expand its membership and improve its services during the years of health-care realignment. Doctors Health Plan is dedicated to improving medical care in the communities it serves. *d*

Within the Veterans Affairs (VA) system, which encompasses 171 medical facilities nationwide, the Durham Veterans Affairs

DURHAM VA MEDICAL CENTER

Medical Center ranks near the top in sheer complexity. The distinction stems from a list of accomplishments that are nearly as complex as the medical center itself: the Durham VA is a tertiary care facility and treats acutely ill veterans; it hosts a number of national programs, including the Quality Management Institute and a Regional Medical Education Center; it boasts the fifth-largest VA research program in the nation; and it is the inaugural location for the VA's National Center for Health Promotion and Disease Prevention. Each VA physician enjoys a dual appointment at nearby Duke University, and more than 70 percent of them participate in funded research. Clearly, the Durham VA Medical Center is at the cutting-edge of health care issues.

The medical center's proud heritage stretches back to 1953, when the first brick structure was built just three and a half miles from downtown Durham on a spacious 18-acre site. Although the location proved fortuitous—across the street from Duke Hospital North, and only a few miles from Durham Regional Hospital—the site is more crowded these days, thanks to a massive expansion completed in 1993.

"To care for him who shall have borne the battle, and for his widow and his orphan."— Durham VA Medical Center

Today's 10-story facility contains 382 tertiary-care beds, with an additional 120-bed, long-term care facility on site. The 1993 addition produced new intensive care units for medicine, surgery, and coronary care, new clinical laboratories, nuclear medicine, and radiology suite. Even a magnetic resonance imaging (MRI) unit was installed.

With state-of-the-

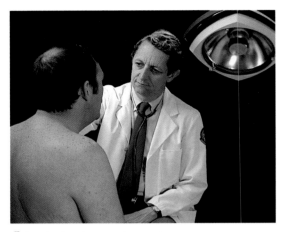

A caring hands-on environment.

art medical equipment and the skills of 1,700 highly trained, compassionate employees, the medical center serves as the medical nerve center for North Carolina's veterans. More than 200,000 veterans in central and eastern North Carolina use the facilities, as well as selected referrals from the mid Atlantic region. The center provides both general and specialty health care, surgical and psychiatric inpatient treatment, and ambulatory services. In addition, a wide variety of specialized treatment programs are offered: geriatrics; stroke and epilepsy; plastic, oral, and maxillofacial surgery; immunology; renal transplants; pancreatic transplants, corneal transplants; open-heart surgery; and radiation therapy. A physician-staffed emergency room is open for acute-care treatment 24 hours a day.

The Home Health Care program, initiated in 1983, calls on a multidisciplinary team of nurses, social workers, and occupational and physical therapists who make house calls to patients residing within a 50-mile radius of the center. This invaluable service provides medical care to veterans who cannot travel to Durham. On the horizon for the medical center is more emphasis on convenient health care access. VA patients in the 29-county service area soon may be able to obtain VA medical services near their own homes in private clinics.

Preventive care is an essential component of any comprehensive medical services package. The Durham VA has established a program that targets disease prevention and health education: the National Center for Health Promotion and Disease Prevention. This new program encourages patients to make choices that can reduce their risk of heart disease or cancer. In addition to education about healthy lifestyles and VA health services, the Center offers evaluation of screening tests for early detection of disease, flu vaccines for elderly veterans, and a national clearinghouse for other facilities in assisting with policy development.

The 120-bed Extended Care and Rehabilitation Center (ECRC), completed in 1990, breaks new ground for the recovering veteran who does not require full hospitalization. Not a nursing home, the ECRC combines the services of an inpatient facility with a rehabilitation hospital. The thrust of rehabilitation treatment involves an integrated effort through nursing, medical, rehabilitative, and psychosocial care. The ultimate goal of ECRC treatment is that patients become self-sufficient by the time they are discharged.

As part of an ongoing effort to expand services to traditionally underserved segments of the veteran population, the Durham VA Medical Center operates a full-service Women's Health Center. The center was designed specifically to improve access of women veterans to health care and state-of-the-art diagnostic and therapeutic programs. The clinic provides overall physical and mental health services in a comforting, welcoming environment. The Women's Health Center medical team includes experts in fields unique to women's health, such as gynecology, breast cancer, and menopause.

To respond to the needs of an increasing number of patients over age 65, the VA Medical Center developed a specialized Geriatric Research Education and Clinical Center. The center distills research, education, and clinical achievements in geriatrics and gerontology to improve knowledge about aging. The net result has been improved quality of care for this significant group of veterans.

Research plays an important part in the life of the Durham VA in other arenas, too. Funding for grants from the National Institute of Health and VA Research exceeds $14 million per year, with more than 300 research projects under way. There is a strong commitment at the VA to encourage today's research in order to better serve tomorrow's patients.

The medical center's commitment to education provides training for about 1,100 students annually through affiliations with 30 colleges and universities. At any one time, more than 300 students train in a wide variety of areas throughout the facility. This involvement in the education of future medical professionals stimulates staff members to refine their own skills and knowledge and thus contribute to high-quality patient care.

The medical center has traditionally benefited from its close association with Duke University. An important result of that affiliation is that all staff physicians hold full- or part-time academic appointments at the university. Ninety-two percent of physicians at the Durham VA are board certified, and 28 percent are board-certified in more than one specialty area.

The Durham VA is recognized nationally for its Regional Medical Education Center, which provides training for VA personnel from five states and Puerto Rico. RMEC headquarters are now in downtown Durham in newly expanded quarters. The VA Center for Quality Management is also part of the Durham VA, adding to its stature as a leader in health care quality.

Patient care, education, and research are the touchstones of the Durham VA Medical Center. Taken separately or in combination, they simply mean, "Putting Veterans First."

An innovative Women's Health Center.

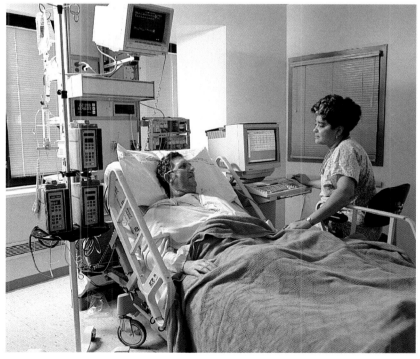

Surgical Intensive Care Unit with electronic medical record.

In 1925, it was considered one of the best liberal arts colleges in America for African-American students. Today, North Carolina Central University (NCCU) looks to its illustrious past to anchor its place in the future of the Research Triangle.

NORTH CAROLINA CENTRAL UNIVERSITY

"Our liberal arts undergraduate program prepares students for entry into graduate and professional schools in our three local universities and employment in research institutions in Research Triangle Park and the nation," said Chancellor Julius Chambers. "Our goal is to be the liberal arts undergraduate university for the Research Triangle Park area."

First on the agenda for NCCU was establishment of higher standards for its students. The university has witnessed an increase in scores on the Scholastic Aptitude Test (SAT). The North Carolina Central University Honors Program supplements classroom work with special projects and activities inspiring students to greater academic effort. "To develop the kinds of programs we want, we have to provide a competitive educational opportunity that prepares our students to measure up to students anywhere," Chambers said.

Chambers' words echo the dream of NCCU's founder, Dr. James E. Shepard. Dr. Shepard spent a year doing Sunday School work in Europe and Africa in 1907, taking careful note of the exceptional educational opportunities for African-Americans. When he returned to Durham he set about establishing a school that would offer high-quality educational programs and religious training for African-Americans. Shepard's National Religious Training School and Chautauqua opened its doors in 1910, with strong support from the Durham community.

Although funding was difficult during the early years, Shepard managed to support the school through private donations and student fees until 1923, when the state assumed financial responsibility for it as a teacher training institution, the Durham State Normal School. Two years later, the school became the North Carolina College for Negroes and offered a substantive liberal arts education that included preparatory courses for secondary school

Conducting an experiment in the Human Science Department (formerly Home Economics).

teachers and principals. North Carolina College for Negroes inaugurated graduate programs in liberal arts and the professions in 1939; the School of Law opened a year later. One of NCCU's most prestigious courses of study—the Master of Library Science—was implemented in 1942.

The institution's name continued to evolve. In 1947, the state legislature declared the school would be known as North Carolina College at Durham. Twenty years later, James Shepard's religious training school became North Carolina Central University. NCCU joined the University of North Carolina System as a constituent institution in 1972.

Today, with a student body of nearly 6,000, NCCU sits at the center of the "Big Three," as Chambers describes the area's other large universities: Duke University, the University of North Carolina at Chapel Hill (UNC), and North Carolina State University. Rather than try to compete against such powerhouse institutions, NCCU and the "Big Three" work cooperatively, a position that enriches all of them.

NCCU's new undergraduate program in environmental science, for instance, complements UNC's ecology curriculum and Duke's School for the Environment. NC Central provides valuable input on the effects of environmental conditions on the health of minorities and the poor. Similarly, NCCU's School of Law fills glaring voids left by the legal profession. "The law school is crucial, because other area law schools don't emphasize the needs of the poor and minorities who can't afford lawyers," Chambers said. Coincidentally, NCCU's Law School offers the only evening degree program

Discussing the finer points of the art of making ceramics in NCCU's Art Department.

in the state, a factor in its overwhelming popularity. Although all three universities offer education degrees, it is NCCU that graduates most of the state's minority teachers. About 100 education majors graduate each year from NCCU; a new School of Education is on the drawing board. NCCU also has stepped up its involvement with international programs, a point of intellectual convergence for all four universities.

Under Chambers' leadership, the university has forged strong links with several RTP firms. The Environmental Protection Agency, one of RTP's largest federal institutions, helped write the curriculum for NCCU's interdisciplinary Environmental Science program. Emerging biomedical and biotechnology programs at NCCU have also piqued the interest of RTP firms. "It's exciting to see how folks involved in biomedical research welcomed NCCU's interest," Chambers said. "With all these efforts, NCCU seeks diversity. We need to reach out to everybody, and we need the facilities and programs to attract everybody."

Innovative programs like biomedical research carry a high price tag, so NCCU has embarked on a round of philanthropic fundraising to supplement state funding. Alumni donations have increased, and benefactors have committed funds for seven endowed chairs. Locally, the university has encouraged 250 Durham businesses to establish a habit of giving.

"Local fund-raising is valid," Chambers said, "since 25 percent of the student body comes from Durham. Many of those students transfer into NCCU or are older, employed adults working toward degrees in their fields." Chambers has extended a helping hand to the

Dressing for success, NCCU students prepare for graduation ceremonies.

Durham community through the Office of Community Services, established in 1994. More than 3,000 students have expressed interest in doing volunteer work with 150 Durham charitable and service agencies. Chambers has proposed that community service be added as a graduation requirement for all NCCU students, the first public university to request mandatory volunteerism.

Certainly, a long list of NCCU graduates has been dedicated to community service: Atlanta Mayor Maynard Jackson, North Carolina Attorney General Michael Easley, former North Carolina Speaker of the House Dan Blue, former North Carolina House Majority Leader Milton Fitch, Jr., Congresswoman Eva Clayton, and many artists, legislators, college presidents, professors, and professional athletes.

Every student who enters NCCU has the potential to make their mark on the world, according to Chambers. "The university's task is to help them do it. We see a kid come in, who has had limited exposure," he said. "We give him that exposure and experience, and he goes out into the world and makes a contribution. All the frustrations are worth it to see that end product."

An NCCU student examines a biological specimen.

DURHAM MEDICAL CENTER

Durham Medical Center is an innovator in the field of health care. Since 1977, when it opened the doors to its first office, Durham Medical Center has been slightly ahead of its time. It established Durham's first urgent-care center long before the concept caught on elsewhere. It is one of the largest general internal medicine group practices in the area. And now, as the health care industry shakes its very foundations, Durham Medical Center has emerged as a model for tomorrow's medical practice: the source of primary care for the entire family.

"With board-certified physicians in internal medicine, family medicine, and pediatrics, we can handle just about any medical issue in one of our three offices," said Ruth Stewart, administrator of Durham Medical Center. "And in the new arena of managed care, we can save money for the patient and the system."

Founded in 1977 by Robert Stewart, M.D., William Uthe, M.D., and Raymond Toler, M.D., Durham Medical Center has witnessed dramatic changes in the medical profession. Once dictated by microspecialization, today's health care climate now demands competent, primary care physicians who are versed in a wide variety of medical issues. Durham Medical Center's staff of board-certified internists meets those criteria. An adults-only specialty, internal medicine is one of the gatekeepers for health care in the 21st century.

When Durham Medical Center joined the Duke University Health System in 1995, pediatricians and family medicine physicians were added to the roster, boosting the capability of the practice. Now infants, children, adolescents, and their families are welcome at Durham Medical Center. "We think this is a great marriage between internal medicine, family practice, and pediatrics," said Stewart. Durham Medical Center also offers geriatric and nursing-home care and accepts Medicare patients.

In 1995, Durham Medical Center opened Patient First, a walk-in treatment clinic that provides medical care seven days a week without appointment. Patient First, family medicine, internal medicine, and pediatrics are located at 1901 Hillandale Road, the headquarters for Durham Medical Center. A second group of internal medicine physicians practices at new offices at 4220 North Roxboro Road. Woodcroft residents enjoy easy access to the Durham Medical Center office at Highway 54 and Southpark Drive.

Durham Medical Center is proud to offer the following services to its patients:
- Well-baby exams
- School physicals
- Immunizations
- Neonatal care
- Routine physicals
- Gynecological exams
- On-site mammograms
- On-site drug testing
- Minor surgery
- Workers comp exams
- On-site lab, rated "excellent"
- Most insurance accepted
- Patient First, walk-in care, 7 days a week

"Count on Durham Medical Center for all your medical needs," said Stewart. "We've been around a long time, and we'll continue to serve Durham with excellent medical care in the future." *d*

❚ 1901 Hillandale Road
Drs. Adams and Stewart

❚ 4220 North Roxboro Road

When the first facility of The United Methodist Retirement Homes opened in Durham in 1955, an atmosphere of love and confidence permeated the warm, attractive facility. The community fostered a sense of independence combined with humor, joy, and a consideration for others. Not surprisingly, residents were happy to call such a place "Home."

The United Methodist Retirement Homes, Inc., related by faith to the North Carolina Annual Conference of The United Methodist Church, has earned respect over the years for its stability and the quality of life enjoyed by its residents.

The Methodist Retirement Community, the first facility of The United Methodist Retirement Homes, was built on a beautiful 40-acre tract of tree-studded, gently rolling hills next to Duke University. Over the years, the increasing number of senior adults has created the need for additional facilities—now in Lumberton, Greenville, Pinehurst, and the newest campus, Croasdaile Village in Durham.

Croasdaile Village is a continuing care retirement community on a large parcel of the more than 1,000-acre Croasdaile Farm, a family farm now being developed as a planned, private residential neighborhood. The picturesque setting is enhanced by the many acres allocated to natural parks and greenways. Croasdaile Village is located conveniently in the city of Durham, yet the rolling meadows, groves of trees, and

peaceful lakes and ponds make the city seem miles away. The natural landscape creates a serene, secure environment that combines the individuality and privacy of beautifully designed homes, spacious cottages, and airy apartments with the camaraderie of a neighborhood. The convenient location puts shopping, medical facilities, and cultural and fun activities within minutes. A full range of services offers complete peace of mind about health care, both now and in the future.

THE UNITED METHODIST RETIREMENT HOMES, INC.

The moderate climate and natural trails and greenways invite a variety of outdoor activities; the wellness center and exercise opportunities promote a healthy lifestyle.

The celebration of life at Croasdaile Village centers around a warm and caring Christian community that embraces persons of all faiths. Opportunities abound for spiritual, social, and physical growth, as individuals or as groups of friends. Planned activities encourage everyone to express their creativity or interest in art, sports, music, gardening, woodworking, and through a treasure trove of crafts and hobbies. Residents may choose from a schedule of concerts, theater, art exhibits, lectures, sporting events, and trips to exciting attractions.

The community spirit at Croasdaile Village is a continuation of a 40-year tradition of stability, loving care, and quality of life enjoyed by residents. Come be a part of this celebration of life!

Long before Durham was known as the City of Medicine, a physician founded an obstetrics and gynecology practice to address the needs of the city's female population. Seventy years later, Durham Obstetrics & Gynecology, P.A. continues to serve Durham's women from its Duke Street based clinical site.

DURHAM OBSTETRICS & GYNECOLOGY, P.A.

"Dr. Norman Bowles started the practice in 1925 and held the fort until Dr. Trogler Adkins came back from World War II in 1945," said Dr. Robert Yowell, one of the senior partners in the practice. "The two of them worked together until 1960 when Dr. Roston Williamson finished his residency at Duke and became the third member. Eight years later, Dr. Yancey Culton joined the practice and Dr. Yowell followed one year later.

Physicians in the practice today include: Yowell; Rudy W. Barker, M.D.; William R. Lambeth, M.D.; Paul S. Andrews, M.D.; Karen H. Clark, M.D.; Anne Marie Connolly, M.D.; and Charles Peete, M.D. Suzanne Hage is the clinic's certified physician's assistant. The medical staff is supported by a health care team that includes clinical nurse specialists, nursing staff, health educators, laboratory staff, and administrative personnel.

Durham OB-GYN is devoted to the specialized care of women and includes obstetrics, gynecology, infertility, and gynecological surgery. Additional services are provided in the areas of genetic counseling, nutrition counseling, family planning, childbirth education, and prenatal and postpartum classes. Laboratory studies, ultrasound, fetal monitoring, and same-day surgery are also offered through the practice.

During his 25-year tenure at Durham OB-GYN, Yowell has witnessed significant changes in the group. An ever-expanding Durham population prompted expansion in facilities. In 1979, Durham Obstetrics & Gynecology moved to a spacious suite of offices in Central Medical Park on North Duke Street. In 1988, the physicians' group opened a satellite office on Highway 54 in southwest Durham to serve the increasing traffic from Research Triangle Park. Physicians rotate from the Central Medical Park office to the satellite office.

Durham OB-GYN principals, in cooperation with other area physicians, opened the Durham Ambulatory Surgical Center in 1985. This out-patient center, the first of its kind in Durham, offered far greater convenience and faster recovery for patients at lower cost.

"The center was a new concept in the Durham area and provided a wide variety of outpatient surgical procedures in a friendly, comfortable atmosphere," Dr. Yowell said. "The facility proved popular with patients and was an example of the cooperation among area physicians that continues today."

Physicians in the practice constantly upgrade their education to stay abreast of the latest research. They also train resident physicians who rotate through Durham Regional Hospital as surgical assistants. In addition, each Durham OB-GYN physician serves as a consulting assistant professor of Obstetrics and Gynecology, either at Duke University School of Medicine or at the University of North Carolina School of Medicine in Chapel Hill.

Durham Obstetrics & Gynecology practices comprehensive health care with an emphasis on prevention, and the staff works closely with patients to ensure the best possible state of health. "Our group and all the other obstetrics and gynecological groups are closely tuned in to the needs of women in the area. We try to provide first-class services, both in the office and in the hospital," said Yowell. "It's fun to participate in a venture like this and watch it grow," he added. "We feel like we're a special part of the City of Medicine." 🖉

Gerard J. Musante, Ph.D.
Founder and Director

Gerard Musante knows first-hand the trials and tribulations of weight control; he struggled himself as an overweight teenager. As a clinical psychologist, however, he sought answers to the eternal question: Why do humans and food have such a difficult relationship? His conclusion was simple, yet direct: although food is for nutrition, too often it is used as a substitute for comfort or support.

Dr. Musante decided to share his findings with those who wanted to lose weight permanently. In 1977 he founded Structure House, a diet "mecca" for thousands of people from all over the country and the world. Today, they come to Durham seeking solutions to their weight problems and, at Structure House, learn how to lose weight through proper diet and exercise and to develop resources for managing weight control at home. Of course, accomplishing those goals isn't always easy. But the Structure House success rate for long-term weight loss—66 percent compared with the national average of 5 percent—is proof that Musante's theory works in practice.

With its attractive campus, comfortable quarters, classrooms, dining rooms, swimming pools, and well-appointed fitness center, Structure House gives the appearance of a state-of-the-art spa; but there's far more to the weight management curriculum than physical fitness. At Structure House, participants delve into the psychological reasons behind overeating. They learn how to substitute other "feel good" activities for food, to develop successful routes to positive self-esteem, and to learn how to say "no" to food cravings.

There are no magic cures at Structure House. Instead, professionals on the staff work closely with participants to create new means of taking charge of health habits. Attitudes about "diet-ing" are replaced with strategies for healthy behavior. In a comfortable environment that feels like home (with none of the temptations!), participants embrace the three building blocks of the Structure House program: nutritional re-education, a wide range of exercise options, and behavior and lifestyle modification.

By keeping a food diary, participants learn that much overeating stems from habit, boredom, and stress. To help change thought patterns about eating, and put those thoughts into practical application, Structure House schedules a full day of activities. Medical supervision, a fitness and conditioning program, psychological support, and nutrition education and guidance take many forms and are tailored for individual needs. For example, a participant might learn how to monitor glucose, exercise in a swimming pool, manage stress, and plan menus to meet the calories-per-day requirement.

Although there are more than 100 weekly activities at Structure House, there's still plenty of time for participants to explore the Durham community. Structure House visitors bring a cosmopolitan presence to the Triangle as they enjoy their surroundings, shop, attend cultural events, and become, for the length of their stay, "locals." Structure House has helped create yet another title for Durham: "Diet Capital of the World!"

Structure House—Internationally renowned center for weight loss and lifestyle management.

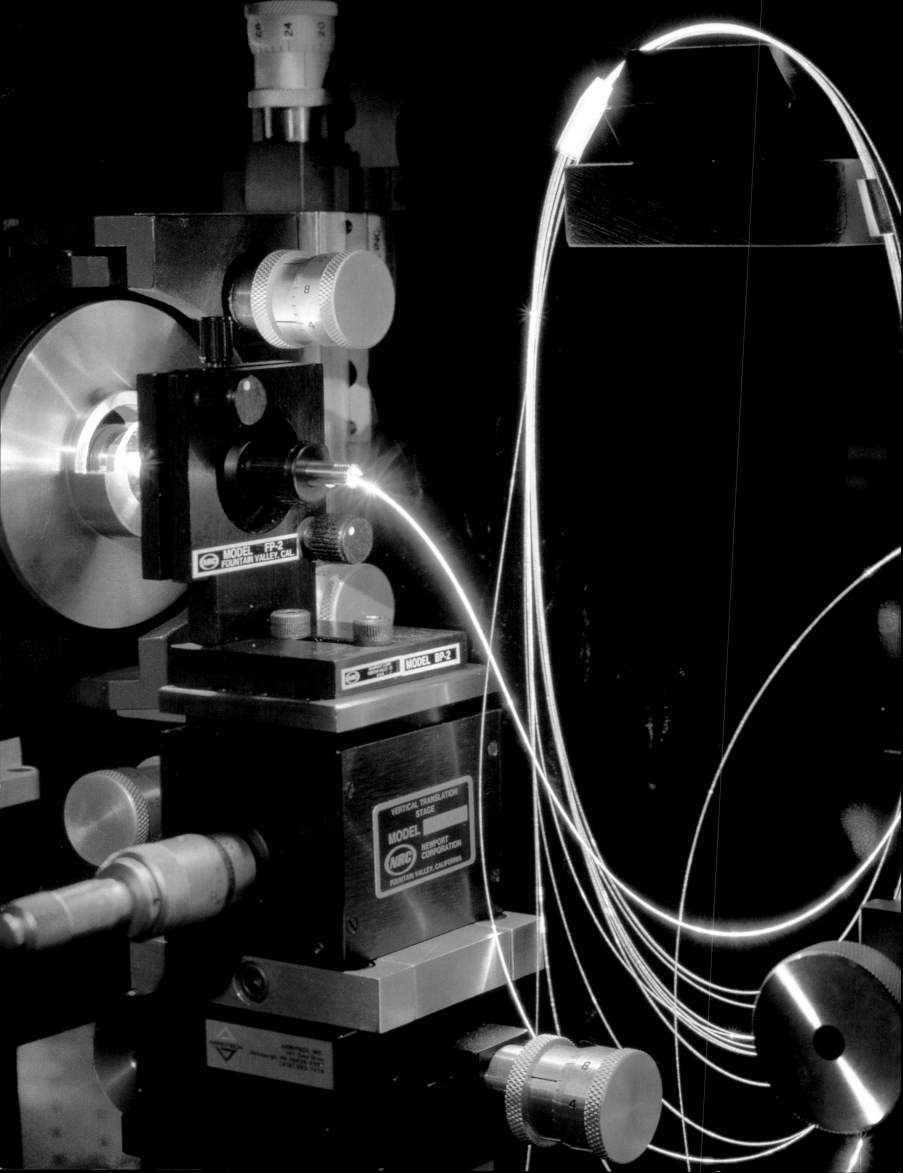

chapter seventeen
17
RESEARCH & TECHNOLOGY

d

Durham, inclusive of Research Triangle Park, leads the nation in the development of cutting-edge research and development that benefits us all. Courtesy of GTE.

Patient satisfaction and an improved quality of life—these are the touchstones that define Glaxo Wellcome Inc. The company has a solid

GLAXO WELLCOME INC.

reputation for producing innovative products to meet diverse medical needs. And although product performance that translates into a strong financial picture is gratifying, people are why Glaxo Wellcome Inc. is in business. Making a personal difference in people's lives is the true bottom line.

Glaxo Wellcome Inc. is the U.S. subsidiary of London-based Glaxo Wellcome plc and the result of the merger of two pharmaceutical giants—Glaxo Inc. and Burroughs Wellcome Co.—in 1995. Glaxo Wellcome plc, the leading pharmaceutical-research company in the world, is an integrated, research-based group of companies whose corporate purpose is to create, discover, develop, manufacture and market throughout the world, safe, effective medicines of the highest quality. These medicines benefit patients through improved longevity and quality of life, and benefit society in general through economic value.

▌ Barbara Long, Senior Chemist, QA Analytical Services, Glaxo Zebulon, checks separations of a Temovate ointment sample using a separatory funnel.

Research Triangle Park (RTP) is home to Glaxo Wellcome Inc.'s headquarters, as well as the company's U.S. research and development facility.

As a responsible corporate citizen, Glaxo Wellcome Inc. has established a policy of giving back a portion of its earnings to the communities in which it operates. As a result, the company is recognized as a major contributor to charities and educational institutions in North Carolina and across the United States.

Glaxo Wellcome concentrates its major research efforts in therapeutic categories that include gastrointestinal, respiratory, antibiotic, antiviral, central nervous system, dermatological and cardiovascular diseases.

At Glaxo Wellcome Inc. it's understood that the discovery of new therapeutic agents is only the beginning. New medicines are created through vision and expertise, coupled with an enormous investment of time and money. And medical miracles aren't cheap. It costs an average of $360 million to bring a new medicine to market, where just three of ten will return a company's investment. And only one of 5,000 new compounds made in the laboratory passes the stringent tests needed to reach a patient's bedside. The success of a new drug isn't based solely on its discovery and development, however. Success comes when the needs of patients are understood in terms of both therapeutic benefits and cost effectiveness.

As research brings forth treatments for many of the diseases plaguing our society, the additional task arises to assure that those medical miracles are delivered at a cost appropriate to the value of the care. Glaxo Wellcome Inc. is at the forefront of this dramatic change and innovative in both the science and the business of health care.

▌ Evening view of R&D Atrium Glaxo Wellcome Inc.

Identifying a medical need and working to create a solution has always been Glaxo Wellcome Inc.'s mission. Today, as the 21st century approaches, company scientists continue to bring innovative ideas to drug research. Glaxo Wellcome Inc. recognizes a fundamental change in the scientific environment, with new technologies, techniques and disciplines offering great opportunities. The company meets the demands of the future with financial strength, a superb research and development capability, an outstanding worldwide staff, and first class manufacturing and marketing capabilities.

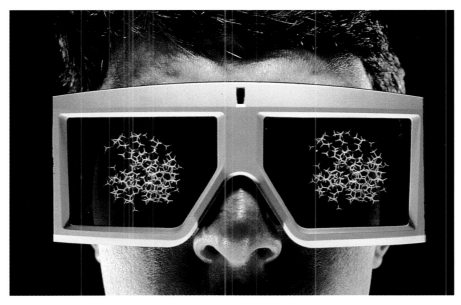

A Glaxo Wellcome researcher using Virtual Reality glasses to look at molecules.

Glaxo Wellcome Inc. is committed, not only to participating in significant change in the pharmaceutical industry, but also to shaping it. A commitment to innovation, a rich product pipeline, a lean infrastructure, and an ability to anticipate and adapt to new business conditions continue to serve the company well. But that doesn't mean wholesale change. Glaxo Wellcome Inc. remains steadfast to its legacy as a research-based company delivering high-quality medicines to people who rely on them. Balancing the needs of society with the needs of the business, Glaxo Wellcome Inc. is committed to uncompromising integrity in its scientific and business practices.

Glaxo Wellcome Inc. will continue to meet the demands of people everywhere for more effective health care, more efficiently provided. To that end, the company depends on the widely varied talents of its employees. Each

of them shares the satisfaction of knowing that every day they inch the world closer toward an end to disease and healthier lives for people. The business of advancing human health and the opportunity to make a difference in the world are the rewards of all the company's employees, from chemists to accountants to engineers and production workers. From the lab to the loading dock, Glaxo Wellcome Inc.'s employees are the company's greatest asset.

The company's mission remains constant— to discover, develop, and market medicines to combat disease and relieve human suffering. Today, Glaxo Wellcome Inc. fulfills that mission by building a competitive worldwide enterprise to succeed in the global marketplace. ⒹⒹ

What does the remote control that runs your television set have in common with your computer keyboard? Both contain microcontrollers

MOTOROLA
SEMICONDUCTOR

—tiny devices found in nearly every type of electronics product. Motorola, the leader in microcontroller sales worldwide, with nearly 20 percent of the market, manufactures them in a semiconductor fabrication facility, or "fab," in the Research Triangle Park.

"Microcontrollers are the working parts of a lot of electronic applications," said Gene

MOS 15, Motorola's Research Triangle Park facility.

Mullinnix, Motorola's site and operations manager. "They're in pagers, microwave ovens, and air bags, as well as in cellular and wireless."

Both microcontrollers and microprocessors are semiconductors, but they differ from one another by their application. While microprocessors are used for high-performance, data-intensive applications, such as personal computers, microcontrollers control the functions of a product, such as deploying an automobile air bag or checking the weight of a load of laundry in a washing machine.

In 1992, there were 148 million microprocessors sold in the world, compared with 1.72 billion microcontrollers. A typical middle-class home has products that use more than 75 microcontrollers; by the end of the century, that number may jump to 250. Everything from

garage door openers to video games are controlled by buttons, voice activation, or other input devices. Software to operate the product is permanently recorded or "embedded" within it, and the microcontroller is invisible to the user.

Motorola's RTP facility, known within the company's network of fabs as MOS 15, is part of the company's aggressive semiconductor manufacturing capacity program. The 150,000-square-foot MOS 15 facility produces additional capacity primarily for Motorola's 8-bit microcontrollers and high-speed logic devices used in communication, automotive, and consumer applications. The fab was acquired from Harris Corporation in July, 1994.

"The early priority decision was to find a factory already operating, with existing staff and demonstrated technological capability," Mullinnix said. "We didn't want to start from scratch and take a number of years to build. This way, we can bring products to the market quicker."

The speed with which products reach the market is important in an industry undergoing explosive change. Chip manufacturers worldwide will build about 50 additional 8-inch wafer fabs before the end of the century. That expansion will meet the needs of companies making products such as multimedia PCs, cellular handsets, and personal digital assistants.

"The semiconductor industry is in the midst of an electronics explosion where there is a great demand for our products," Mullinnix said. "Motorola is diligently working to create more capacity to meet our customers' needs."

The MOS 15 fabrication facility originally was completed in 1982 by General Electric and was acquired by Harris Corporation in 1989. The facility had served primarily as a foundry for Motorola; Harris continued to invest in improvements before it was sold.

Motorola came to RTP with the intention of establishing a long-term presence. In addition to the existing facility, the area had the necessary professional and technical workers and a strong infrastructure that included universities

Peter Lynch and Gene Mullinnix.

and technical and training colleges. Nearly all the former Harris employees were hired as part of the acquisition; within six months, the facility increased employment by 41 percent. The company invested millions of dollars in the RTP facility to expand the existing clean room, purchase new equipment, make infrastructure and process flow improvements, and create approximately 175 new jobs. "And as we continue to expand and equip this facility, the Research Triangle Park will also benefit," Mullinnix said.

The benefit is mutual. Motorola has a good rapport with its RTP neighbors and has built a professional relationship that allows it to offer analytical and manufacturing experience and receive technical advice. Motorola employees serve on the boards of several community organizations and are in advisory roles in community colleges. The company supports the Durham Public Schools through a program that uses its equipment and expertise.

"The speed with which we settled here was a pleasant surprise," Mullinnix said. "We have easily acclimated ourselves, both personally and professionally. And we've achieved a lot in the community to be as new as we are."

Motorola recognizes that an aggressive, semiconductor manufacturing capacity expansion program is vital to the future of the semiconductor industry. The company's Semiconductor Products Sector (SPS), of which MOS 15 is a part, is the largest U.S.-based broad line supplier of semiconductors, with more than 50,000 devices. SPS sales in 1994 were $6.9 billion, nearly a third of Motorola's total sales of $22.2 billion. Motorola is the second-largest semiconductor manufacturer in the world.

Founded in 1928 as Galvin Manufacturing Corporation by brothers Paul and Joseph Galvin, Motorola first produced a battery eliminator that allowed battery-powered home radios to operate on household current. Next came car radios and later, television sets and transistor radios before Motorola concentrated on electronics and communications devices. Company headquarters remained in Schaumburg, Illinois, and other divisions were located in Phoenix, Arizona, and Austin, Texas. Motorola employs about 120,000 people.

The company is one of the leading suppliers of wireless communications and electronic equipment, systems, components, and services for worldwide markets. Motorola makes more cellular phones than any other company in the world and is a leader in the manufacture of pagers. The markets for both cellular phones and pagers are expected to triple by the end of the century.

Other Motorola products include two-way radios, personal communications systems, automotive and industrial electronics, computers, data communications, and information processing and handling equipment. Also, Motorola is developing microcontrollers using the PowerPC, the heart of a new generation of high-speed processors that will be used in applications as diverse as personal computer systems and automobile drive train control. [d]

Motorola workers.

"A lean, mean organization with a high degree of commitment from its workers"—that's how Gerhard Koenig describes

CORMETECH, INC.

Cormetech, Inc. The company's team-based management system translates into a motivated work force that delivers cutting-edge, high-quality environmental products.

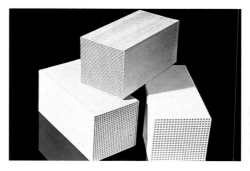

■ SCR Cormetech Honeycomb Catalysts.

"We have various manufacturing operations, and each one is handled by team members who make decisions on how to get the job done," said Koenig, Cormetech's president and chief executive officer. "We're not the traditional hierarchical organization."

Cormetech, Inc. isn't the traditional manufacturing company, either. The environmental technologies firm designs and manufactures ceramic-based honeycomb catalysts that cost effectively remove 90 percent or more of nitrogen oxides (NO) from stationary combustion systems that burn fossil fuels. Nitrous oxide emissions are removed by the Selective Catalytic Reduction (SCR) process whose key components are Cormetech's catalysts. In the SCR process, ammonia injected in the flue gas, reacts with nitrogen oxides in the presence of a catalyst, converting the oxides into harmless nitrogen and water.

"Our business stems from legislation—the Clean Air Act and its 1990 Amendment," Koenig said. "We supply Cormetech's catalysts to electric utilities, petroleum refineries, and chemical manufacturers so they can comply with the new laws."

Because not every flue-gas stream is the same, each product Cormetech delivers is custom-engineered to fit a specific application and site. Company personnel supervise installation and conduct follow-up testing. In-house pilot testing capability allows engineers to simulate customers' actual flue-gas conditions and provide reliable data on catalytic performance.

Since it began manufacturing in 1992, Cormetech's primary market has been in California, a state that already has strict air emis-

■ Cormetech, Inc.

sions standards. The company has expanded capacity once to meet increased demand and may boost production again, as eastern states begin to grapple with compliance issues.

Cormetech, Inc. is a joint-equity company of Corning and Mitsubishi. Corning is a leader in extrusion processes for ceramic honeycombs in the automotive emission-control field. Mitsubishi and its licensees have supplied nearly half the SCR systems used on utility and industrial boilers as well as combustion turbines throughout the world.

The equity company, created in 1989, spent its first years in market development. Then it began an extensive manufacturing site-selection process across the eastern United States. When company officials visited Treyburn Corporate Park in northern Durham County, they were impressed by the site's easy access to the Raleigh-Durham International Airport and major highways. The Triangle's work force caliber and the support received from the community convinced Koenig that Treyburn was the right place to build.

Finding just the right employees for a manufacturing company like Cormetech is vital to its success. Cormetech works closely with the Durham Technical Community College offering job training for recruits. A unique pay-for-skill reward method allows workers to earn more money as they master new job skills. "We do a lot of training," Koenig said. "But we have a core group of people now who know each step in the process and can be moved around to help with the training task and to accommodate the order load."

Cormetech, Inc. enjoys an unusual depth of resources, a state-of-the-art manufacturing facility and testing lab, and the experience of installations operating successfully in Japan and Europe. The sum total means reliability, flexibility, technical excellence, and value for Cormetech customers. ✍

DuPont's electronic materials allow you to defrost your car's rear window.

cializes in chemicals and energy, operating more than 200 manufacturing/processing facilities in 40 countries. DuPont is rated one of the top 50 industrial companies in the world and reports annual sales of about $40 billion. It is also one of the oldest continuously operating industrial enterprises in the nation.

DUPONT

The company was established in 1802 by French immigrant Eleuthére Irénée (E.I.) du Pont de Nemours near Wilmington, Delaware. Du Pont de Nemours brought new ideas about the manufacture of gun and blasting powder to America and set up the first "manufactory." At the beginning of the 20th century, the company was bought by three du Pont grandsons—Thomas Coleman du Pont, Alfred I. du Pont, and Pierre Samuel du Pont.

The new owners began to seek out other kinds of business and create new products through research. By World War II, DuPont had developed a strong foundation in polymer science, which led to profitable businesses in fibers, films, plastic resins, and finishes. Today, the company has evolved far from its original business and metamorphosed many times. Its markets now include aerospace, agriculture, apparel, automotive, construction, electronics, energy, and packaging. One thing remains constant as DuPont approaches its third century—a commitment to high quality in the production of "better things for better living."

In the 1930s, DuPont scientists perfected the art of applying gold leaf to the rim of a piece of fine china. Today, that technique has been adapted for a quite different purpose: to silkscreen ink onto car windows as defrosters, for example. Innovative evolution of technology —in this case, from dishes to automobiles—is a DuPont trademark.

At the DuPont Electronics Technology Center in the Research Triangle Park (RTP), the emphasis is on electronic materials. From the RTP center, DuPont creates cutting-edge technology that finds its way into everyday products: cordless telephones, laptop computers, and notebook calculators. DuPont electronic circuits tell an antilock brake system when to engage, and they even help the medical staff read electrocardiograms.

DuPont's RTP facility also meets the challenges of the printed wiring-board industry. It offers custom materials and services to its clients, usually manufacturers of electrical and electronic circuits and components. That preoccupation with satisfying customers, coupled with the highest standards of integrity, bespeaks the very essence of DuPont.

The research and technology company spe-

Wherever DuPont employees are found—from Research Triangle Park to Asia and Europe—the company prides itself on being a global enterprise viewed as a local business. This concept is the springboard for a corporate philanthropic program targeted to the special needs of each of DuPont's local communities. The company contributes $30 million a year to programs that improve the education, quality of life, and economic vitality of those communities.

The RTP area, as well as the rest of DuPont's communities, agree with customers, investors, employees, and suppliers that DuPont is a good company to buy from, invest in, work for, sell to, and have as a neighbor.

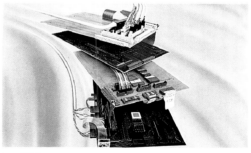

DuPont's electronic materials are used for printed circuit boards at the heart of every computer and electronic device.

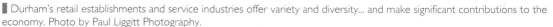
Durham's retail establishments and service industries offer variety and diversity... and make significant contributions to the economy. Photo by Paul Liggitt Photography.

chapter eighteen 18

THE MARKETPLACE

d

BELK LEGGETT COMPANY

It was a daring innovation for its time: to pay cash for retail inventory, mark it up only a small amount, attach a fixed price, then sell on a cash-only basis. The concept defied the longstanding traditions of haggling over prices and buying on credit, but shop owner William Henry Belk offered yet another astonishing promise: satisfaction guaranteed or your money back!

From that first 1,500-square-foot storefront that opened its doors in 1888 in Monroe, North Carolina, Belk created a retailing network, firmly rooted in providing customer service and quality merchandise. Today, there are nearly 350 Belk and Leggett stores in 17 southeastern states, still extolling a vision identical to their founders—and with good reason. Many of the contemporary descendants of that original Belk's store are owned and operated by descendants or heirs of the original principals in the company.

Instead of a megacorporate structure, Belk and Leggett stores are loosely connected through a collection of separate smaller corporations, often owned by different stockholders. This organization gives the company the flexi-bility to accommodate local markets, making it truly a hometown department store for each community it serves.

Nowhere is the hometown flavor more apparent than in Durham and the Triangle, where Belk Hudson Leggett has more than one million square feet of retail space. There are a total of 1,300 employees who work in 10 stores throughout Durham, Chapel Hill, Raleigh, and Cary, and the surrounding communities. Durham boasts two Belk Leggett stores: the South Square Mall location has long been a favorite of savvy shoppers; a new Northgate Mall store opened in 1995, offering extra convenience for shoppers who travel the I-85 corridor. Northgate's 104,000-square-foot facility was designed for the 21st century, catering to the lifestyles of busy, well-educated consumers.

Hudson Belk has been a fixture in the Triangle since 1915, when K. G. Hudson explored his new sales territory on horseback! The 25-year-old Hudson, a seasoned retailer with experience at Hudson stores in Waxhaw, reported strong potential for department stores in the region. A Raleigh store opened first, quickly followed by stores in Durham, Smithfield, Fuquay, and Rocky Mount. William Henry Belk's brother, John, joined the firm, and the company grew rapidly; by 1928, there were 41 stores. When William Henry Belk died in 1952, the retailing empire had grown to 300 stores.

As the stores prospered, some were sold to their dedicated managers; others affiliated with the corporate organization. Every store, regardless of ownership, maintained the staunch Belk-inspired tradition of providing the best value for customers. The markups were small; likewise, the sales were conservative. Those principles held the stores to a fair margin of profitability through the exuberant 1920s and allowed them to remain open even during the years of the Great Depression.

Belk stores broke new ground for retailers in the late 1800s when William Belk ordered an ambitious advertising campaign. In an era when advertising was front-page news, the message was heard loud and clear: "Cheap Goods Sell Themselves!" Fifty years later, Belk stores would offer a live pony as a prize during its back-to-school sales promotion. The company was among the first to establish its own

From the mall, customers have a first glimpse of a well-lighted, spacious store. Photo by Ray Barbour.

The Northgate Mall store can be easily accessed from I-85. Photo by Ray Barbour.

advertising department in the 1950s.

Of course, advertising is useless without a strong line of products, attractively presented to customers. Belk Hudson Leggett stores are noted for their outstanding merchandise. Buyers stay abreast of local and national market trends so that stores are stocked with fashionable, quality brands such as Ralph Lauren, Estee Lauder, and Waterford.

All year round, Belk Hudson Leggett customers are treated like royalty. In yesteryear, customers were invited into the store the day before a sale to preview the merchandise. Today, customers are treated to more efficient services: interest-free 30-60-90-day charge accounts; free alterations on clothing; a bridal registry (featured in *Brides* magazine); package delivery; free gift wrap; gift certificates; and personal fashion and gift consultants.

To further ensure strong service for customers, the stores have implemented a program of professional sales training. Apparently, emphasis on customer satisfaction has been effective. *Consumer Reports* magazine recently rated the stores among the top 10 stores in the nation for excellent service. Locally, the Belk Hudson Leggett store at South Square Mall was named first in quality customer service by the Greater Durham Chamber of Commerce.

The focus on local service doesn't stop at the mall entrance. Belk Hudson Leggett owners, managers, and employees contribute to community projects and charities, as well as their own churches, often giving a substantial portion of their profits. The famed Duke Children's Classic and Durham United Way are among the beneficiaries of their largesse.

Times have certainly changed since William Belk opened his small store in 1888, but at today's Belk Hudson Leggett stores, customers are still treated with integrity, honesty, and fairness. A few basic principles remain intact: customers are received with courtesy and interest; every effort is made to conduct transactions efficiently and promptly; and exchanges and refunds are handled willingly. William Henry Belk would have approved. ▐d▌

▌ Exciting cosmetic displays highlight the South Square store's mall entrance. Photo by Ray Barbour.

Durham has a wealth of medical facilities, research opportunities, educational organizations, and cultural attractions that make it a

OMNI DURHAM HOTEL & DURHAM CIVIC CENTER

popular destination for both business people and vacationers. Located in the heart of downtown is the Omni Durham Hotel and Durham Civic Center, the most unique facility of its kind in the Triangle. Offering both a 187 room luxury hotel and 40,000 square feet of meeting space, it provides excellent service and a pleasant atmosphere for professional meetings, banquets, and conventions.

The Omni Durham Hotel and Durham Civic Center opened on Foster Street in 1989. The complex is just four miles from the Research Triangle Park, a mile from North Carolina Central University, and minutes from Duke University's expansive campus. RDU International Airport, the University of North Carolina at Chapel Hill, and North Carolina State University are also easily accessible from the city center.

Durham, with neighboring Chapel Hill and Raleigh/Cary, anchors a region ranked as the number one place to do business in the nation. In addition, it is located within an hour's flight or a day's drive from 54 percent of the nation's population. The city has the capacity to accomodate 85 to 90 percent of the nation's meeting business and hosts 5,000 conventions and meetings, which attract 200,000 delegates annually.

Before, during, and after meetings, delegates can enjoy many historic sites, arts centers, baseball, and basketball—all within easy reach of the Omni Durham Hotel and Durham Civic Center. An attractive feature of the hotel complex is its location within Durham's arts, entertainment, and historic district, together with the Carolina Theatre, the Durham Arts Council, and the Durham Armory.

Easily accessible through the Durham Civic Center is the Carolina Theatre on Morgan Street. The theatre reopened in 1994 after extensive renovations that restored it to its original 1920's decor. An auditorium for live performances, which include dance, music, and drama, plus the two cinemas, make the Carolina the perfect place to unwind after hours.

The Durham Arts Council, home to theaters, galleries, and arts classes, is located next door to the Carolina Theatre on Morris Street. Hotel guests can browse through art exhibits or catch a local theatrical or musical performance. Across Foster Street from the Omni Durham Hotel is the Durham Armory, a mainstay of downtown Durham and a favorite spot for local celebrations and gala events.

The Omni Durham Hotel and Durham Civic Center's cooperation with the Carolina Theatre, the Durham Arts Council, and the Durham Armory, provides unparalleled flexibility, convenience, and charm for meetings, large and small. In addition to 14,000 square feet of ballroom space, there's 18,000 square feet of column-free exhibit space, 10 meeting rooms that include 2 executive boardrooms, and a full-service restaurant and bar right in the Omni Durham Hotel lobby.

Although it sits in the center of downtown Durham, the hotel and civic center complex has created a small, cooling oasis in its plaza and lobby areas. The spacious plaza contains several fountains and the hotel lobby is light and airy. A pre-function area adjoining the lobby provides easy access to ballrooms, meeting rooms, and exhibit halls. At the end of a busy day, the Omni Lounge is the perfect place for cocktails and conversation.

A successful meeting or event always includes some free-time activities, and they're

▌The Omni Cafe.

Twilight at the Omni.

in abundance in the vicinity of the Omni Durham Hotel and Durham Civic Center. So, whether you've come to meet, sleep, shop, or sightsee, there's plenty to do in or near downtown Durham.

A delectable sampling of local cuisine is available at more than 15 restaurants within a six-block radius of the hotel and civic center. Brightleaf Square, just five blocks from the Omni, is a much-admired collection of unique shops gathered into an elegant, renovated tobacco warehouse. Antiques, clothes, books, jewelry, and gourmet food are all available in this one-of-a-kind shopping venue. Three large department stores and 140 other shops are in Northgate Mall, about a mile from the Omni, and the hotel is happy to provide free transportation to and from the mall for its guests.

Visit the Duke University campus for a glimpse of stunning Gothic architecture and beautiful gardens. From April through October, catch a Durham Bulls baseball game at the team's new stadium. If museums are in your travel plans, don't miss the North Carolina Museum of Life and Science, the Duke University Museum of Art, and the North Carolina Central University Art Museum. St. Joseph's Cultural Center has art

galleries and classes related to African-American culture.

The Omni Durham Hotel and Durham Civic Center serves the local community through its involvement in such events as CenterFest, Durham's festival of the arts held downtown each September. This street party and fair, which gets bigger each year, features vendors, performers, and exhibits that attract 65,000 people. The hotel and civic center complex also plays host to the Software Developers' Competition, initiated in 1991 by a Durham businessman, which draws participants from all over the world. The Civic Center Plaza hosts Durham Alive, a free concert series sponsored by downtown businesses during the summer months.

So, whether it's a quick business trip, an extended family vacation, or a full-fledged convention, the Omni Durham Hotel and Durham Civic Center is your best bet for lodging, meeting room, and banquet facilities. *d*

Executive boardroom.

South Square Mall has a well-deserved reputation of being the best place to shop in Durham and Chapel Hill. The 20-year-old mall

SOUTH SQUARE MALL

is the only two level mall in the immediate area and offers a comfortable sense of spaciousness, easy access to major highways, 4,500 parking spaces, and excellent stores.

South Square Mall is positioned in one of the most enviable trade locations in the Triangle. It commands a prime position between Duke University and the town of Chapel Hill, home of the University of North Carolina. The Research Triangle Park, with its more than 34,000 employees, is just 10 miles away. Fifty thousand cars pass the mall each day on the 15-501 business corridor that links I-85 and I-40. With *Money* magazine's recent ranking of Raleigh/Durham/Chapel Hill as the "Best Place to live in America", South Square is uniquely the best place to shop in the Triangle.

The mall's anchor department stores include the largest Belk-Leggett, Dillard's, and J.C. Penney stores in Durham and Chapel Hill. Other popular stores include Eddie Bauer, Structure, The Gap, Gap Kids, Limited, Limited Too, Sharon Luggage & Gifts, Wilson's Suede and Leather, Moondance Gallery, and The White House. A comfortable, and convenient food court offers a variety of places to enjoy an entire meal or a quick snack.

South Square prides itself on being a customer-service oriented mall. The Customer Service Center, located on the lower level, offers gift certificates, gift wrapping, stroller rental, fax and copier services, wheelchairs, TCD for hearing impaired information services, and a personal gift registry.

South Square Mall has earned a reputation as a safe mall, with an established security force that's been on the job for 15 years. Although customers agree that security, convenience, and

selection are important when they choose a mall, South Square is probably best known for its holiday displays.

▌ The White House.

South Square Mall's Christmas and Easter decor is legendary and draws visitors from far beyond just the Triangle area. Mall employees design and build magnificent sets that are uniquely different each year, delighting adults and children alike. And speaking of those smallest shoppers, the season isn't complete without a visit to Santa's Magic Castle at South Square Mall— THE place to be at Christmas, or any time of the year! ▨

▌ Center Court Fountain at
South Square Mall.

When you discover the Sheraton Inn University Center, a well-established hotel in a pleasant suburban setting, you've discovered a home away from home. A friendly and experienced staff anticipates your needs and maintains the high level of service you and your fellow guests have come to expect.

The Sheraton is located near Duke University and Duke University Medical Center, so alumni and faculty, as well as participants in university functions, are frequent hotel guests. Front-door access to I-85 brings North Carolina Central University, the University of North Carolina at Chapel Hill, and the Research Triangle Park within minutes of the Sheraton. And the Raleigh-Durham International Airport is an easy 15-minute trip.

The Durham icon opened in 1982 and is Durham's second-largest hotel. Its 225-member staff is adept at playing host to those who visit for graduations, weddings, and conferences. With 16,000 square feet of meeting space in 17 meeting rooms, the Sheraton Inn University Center is also a choice site for conventions. The hotel has 315 large sleeping rooms, 70 percent of them nonsmoking and several accessible for handicapped guests.

Special attention and services are offered to guests of the Sheraton's fourth-floor Chancellors Quarters. Breakfast in the Chancellors Quarters is the perfect way to begin the day. Then, when business demands take precedence, fax machines and printers are provided. Magazines, newspapers, and televi-

sion sets are available for those who want to catch up on the day's news.

Downstairs, Sheraton guests can relax in the comfort of Queen Anne chairs and enjoy complimentary hors d'oeuvres in the first-floor Varsity Lounge. Cathedral ceilings and a warm fireplace give this lobby bar special ambience. Praline's Restaurant, in the best tradition of the Old South, offers casual dining in an intimate setting that overlooks the patio and gazebo. Praline's Carolina Cuisine, during the lavish holiday brunches or for visits to the restaurant, is a popular choice for visitors and local residents.

Amenities, which make a stay at the Sheraton Inn University Center memorable, include an indoor swimming pool, health and fitness facilities, an indoor whirlpool, and a gift shop. The Sheraton spa entices guests with full-body massages, waxing, manicures, and pedicures—even a hairstylist. For a high-energy workout, the hotel offers transportation to and from the challenging Duke University jogging trail.

Never content to rest on its well-deserved laurels, the Sheraton completed a $2 million renovation during the summer of 1995. Guest rooms were updated with new wallpaper, carpeting, drapes, and fixtures. The hotel's twin ballrooms were fitted with divider walls and new carpeting. And state-of-the-art keylock and telephone systems, and the newly refurbished lobby and bar/restaurant areas were all part of the renovation.

Business and leisure travelers alike find a warm welcome at the Sheraton Inn University Center. The staff takes pleasure in pampering its customers as special guests. ◨

177

NORTHGATE MALL

Northgate Mall's theme for dedication of the new wing that opened in the fall of 1994 was actually a rededication to the principles Northgate Associates Limited Partnership has upheld throughout its 35-year history.

"Quality, style, value, convenience, community, and fun. We feel very strongly about being able to provide all those to our customers," said Virginia Rand Bowman, general partner in the partnership.

Bowman shares partnership duties of the Northgate Associates Limited Partnership with her father, W. Kenan Rand, Jr., who founded Northgate Mall in the early 1960s. Then, the fledgling mall was a simple strip shopping center. Today, the Northgate shopping complex encompasses approximately 900,000 square feet of enclosed mall space and a 47,000-square-foot Convenience Center. There are more than 150 retail stores and services, and pedestrian traffic averages over 100,000 per week.

Appropriately enough, the new addition to the mall was constructed on the same site as the original strip shopping center. Hecht's department store, a division of the May Company of St. Louis, relocated into 150,000 square feet of the new space, anchoring the wing. Belk Hudson Leggett has opened in the 104,000-square-foot space formerly occupied by Hecht's.

When the partners decided to convert the strip center into a mall in 1974, the two main anchor stores were Sears and Thalhimers (now Hecht's). "The anchor stores have been our biggest achievements over the years and the forces around which development has occurred," Bowman said. Thalhimers doubled in size in 1987 and relocated three times within the shopping complex before being bought out by the May Company in 1991. Sears completed a major renovation project last year.

Over 20 new stores opened in Northgate's new wing in October, 1994.

The Northgate Shopping Complex is located on I-85, the north-south transportation corridor through the Southeast. This strategic location draws customers from all over Durham, as well as those who come to shop from as far north as the Virginia border and as far west as Burlington.

A handful of smaller stores has been part of the mall since it opened: DSG Sports, The Curtain Shop, and Wills Book Store. Bowman said the mall had a variety of unique local merchants that gave it a special flavor. "We're not an `anywhere' mall," she said. "We have a large number of independent and regional merchants. We are continually growing, upgrading, and trying to enhance our existing merchandise mix."

As a locally owned and operated mall, Northgate Associates welcomes community and charity events and provide space for non-profit organizations. In 1990, a carousel was added to attract young families and provide entertainment for children, and the Northgate Express has become a Christmas-season tradition. Durham schools display art work in the mall, and cultural events take place regularly.

A four-year-old frequent shopper program is designed to build customer loyalty and increase shopping frequency. Customers earn privileges and premiums through the program, and the mall offers special benefits that relate to their lifestyles. Northgate Mall sees such niche marketing as vital in an area that continues to grow rapidly in both the residential and commercial sectors. "We are fortunate to be in the Research Triangle area," Bowman said. "However, one thing you can't do is kick your feet up, relax, and rest on your laurels."

A unique relationship between the Hampton Inn on Hillandale Road and Duke University Medical Center's bone marrow transplant program has benefited both hotel and hospital. The real beneficiaries, however, are the breast cancer patients who call the hotel "home" while they're receiving treatment at the bone marrow clinic next door.

The hotel-hospital partnership has made the bone marrow program accessible to patients, who spend about six weeks taking treatment at the clinic. Exchanging the hospital environment for that of a hotel can increase a patient's well-being and accelerate recovery, according to Timothy Carnes, the Hampton Inn's general manager.

"Lifting the spirits is a big part of the battle for these guests," he said. "It's satisfying to contribute to someone's life being saved, and it's a rare opportunity when a hotel can do that."

These guests, who occupy 14 specially furnished rooms at the Hampton Inn year-round, are treated as VIPs in the hotel. Staff members take a special interest in these guests. The hotel offers the VIP's rooms with recliners, microfridges, and hair dryers; washers and dryers are conveniently located in the spa, plus a special 5th-floor VIP lounge. These amenities add up to a very special experience for guests who need long-term accommodations.

Other visitors, in town for business or pleasure, are also treated royally at the Hampton Inn. A diverse group of 137 rooms, including mini-suites, is available to guests. Fifty rooms have microfridges, and 30 rooms have champagne tubs—so named because they blow fresh air bubbles into the water. A deluxe breakfast is served in the lobby each morning, and shuttle service is available 16 hours a day. A security system controls access at all entrances after dark and protects guests by requiring voice and visual identification.

A hospitality suite featuring a large table that seats 10; a seating area with a couch, two chairs, and a cocktail table; a solid oak wall bed system with a king size bed, built-in desk and beautiful glass shelves; a TV with built-in VCR; a kitchenette with microwave and refrigerator; a champagne tub and hairdryer are also available for guests who are looking for the perfect upgraded room.

The Hampton Inn, which opened on Hillandale Road in 1987, is one of 21 hotels in the Winston Hospitality Group. Keeping the hotel in tip-top shape is a high priority for the Hampton Inn; the hotel reinvests 5 percent of its revenues each year in upgrades and renewal. The hotel has undergone two major renovations since opening day.

The Hampton Inn's 38-member staff keeps the hotel running smoothly and takes care of the needs of all its guests. Such attention to the comfort of its customers earned the Hampton Inn one of the highest occupancy rates in North Carolina.

"If you run a good hotel, you can command the available market," Carnes said. "But you have to recognize the needs of your customers and adjust to those needs. We've adjusted our product to what our customers want, and the result is a hotel that's consistent and hospitable seven days a week."

BIBLIOGRAPHY

Anderson, Jean. *Durham County* Durham: Duke University Press, 1990.

Centennial Issue of THE DURHAM SUN. "A Shining Century." 1989.

Dixon, Wyatt. *How Times Do Change*. Durham: Central Carolina Press, 1987.

"Duke University Basketball Yearbook." Duke University Department of Athletics and The Sports Information Office, 1994.

Durden, Robert. *The Dukes of Durham*. Durham: Duke University Press, 1987.

Durden, Robert. *Launching of Duke University*. Durham: Duke University Press, 1993.

Durham Convention and Visitors Bureau. OFFICIAL VISITORS GUIDE.

Durham County Library. DURHAM COMMUNITY RESOURCES. 1993.

"Economic Survey." Durham Chamber of Commerce, 1994.

Flowers, John Baxton, III. *Bull Durham and Beyond*. Durham Bicentennial Commission, 1976.

Hergot, J. Barlow and Katherine Kopp. *Insiders Guide to the Triangle*. Becklyn Publishing Group, Inc., 1994.

Holloway, Betsey. *Heaven for Beginners*. Orlando: Persimmon Press, 1994.

Holloway, Betsey. *Unfinished Heaven*. Orlando: Persimmon Press, 1994.

Kostyu, Joel and Frank Kostyu. *A Pictorial History of Durham*. Durham: Kinship Press, 1992.

Larrabee, Charles X. *Many Missions*. Durham: Research Triangle Institute, 1991.

Leyburn, James G. *Way We Lived, Durham 1900-1920*. Elliston, VA: Northcross House, 1989.

Lougee, George Jr. *Durham, My Hometown*. Durham: Carolina Academic Press, 1990.

"Park Guide." LEADER MAGAZINE. Raleigh: Village Publishing, 1989-1994.

Reynolds, P. Preston, MD, Ph.D. and Joe Liles. *Watts Hospital of Durham, NC*. The Fund for the Advancement of Science and Mathematics Education in North Carolina, 1991.

Reynolds, P. Preston. *Watts Hospital 1895-1976 Paternalism and Race: the Evolution of a Southern Institution in Durham, NC*. Durham: Thesis-Duke University Press.

Roberts, Claudia, Diane Lea, Robert Leary. *Durham Architectural and Historic Inventory*. The City of Durham, North Carolina, 1994.

"Triangle Business Journal, 1994-95," (Book of Lists).

▌ Photo by Paul Liggitt Photography.

ACKNOWLEDGMENTS

Many thanks to the people who helped create this book:

Bill Baucom, Durham Chamber of Commerce

William V. Bell

Bob Booth, Durham Chamber of Commerce

Reyn Bowman, Durham Convention and Visitors Bureau

Don Brady, Durham County Hospital Corporation

Dr. Julius Chambers, North Carolina Central University

William and Josephine Clement

William Coman

Dr. Eugene Eaves, North Carolina Central University

Dr. John Friedrick, North Carolina School of Science and Mathematics

Carleton Harrell, Durham Herald Sun

Bonnie Harris, Managing Editor

Becky Heron, Durham Board of County Commissioners

Bill Kalkhof, Downtown Durham, Inc.

Nannerl Keohane, Duke University

Sylvia Kerckhoff, Mayor of Durham

Charles X. Larrabee

Richard Myers, Durham County Hospital Corporation

Carol Myrick

Paul Norby, Durham City/County Planning

Judy Older, Prudential Carolinas Realty

Dr. Owen Phillips, Durham Public Schools

Jim Roberson, Research Triangle Foundation

Ralph Snyderman, Duke University Medical Center

Larry Suitt, Durham County Hospital Corporation

Dr. Thomas Wooten, Research Triangle Institute

Dr. LeRoy Walker, Jr., US Olympic Committee

Tom White, Greater Durham Chamber of Commerce

—and the many others who contributed their time and expertise.

Special gratitude to my loving family and eternally patient friends
who kept a candle in the window for me during those long months of
research, interviews, writing, and editing.

DURHAM'S ENTERPRISES

DURHAM'S ENTERPRISES

INDEX

INDEX

INDEX

INDEX

❚ Cover photos, page 2 and page 4 photos by Paul Liggitt Photography.
❚ Page 8. Photo by Bob Hopkins/Impact Photography.
❚ Page 10. Photo by Paul Liggitt Photography.
❚ Page 12. Photo by Paul Liggitt Photography.
❚ Page 96. Photo by Paul Liggitt Photography.
❚ Page 107. Photo by Paul Liggitt Photography.
❚ Page 143. Courtesy of *Herald Sun Newspapers*. Photo by Grant Halverson.

This book was set in Palatino, Spring Light, Caslon Open Face
and Gill San Light at Community Communications, Inc., Montgomery, Alabama
and printed on 80 lb. Warren Flo Text.